ALSO BY THE AUTHOR

Vegetarian Dishes from Around the World

The Festive Vegetarian

The Festive Vegetarian

Recipes and Menus for Every Occasion

by
Rose Elliot

Pantheon Books
New York

Library of Congress Cataloging in Publication Data
Elliot, Rose.
Vegetarian feasts.
Reprint. Originally published: Gourmet vegetarian cooking.
London: W. Collins Sons, 1982.
Includes index.
1. Vegetarian cookery. 2. Menus. I. Title.
TX 837. E43 1983   641.5'636   82-19097
ISBN 0-394-71402-4

Manufactured in the United States of America
First American Edition
Book design: Elissa Ichiyasu

To Anthony, with love and thanks

Contents

Introduction

Gourmet cooking means food that truly satisfies the senses: food in which the balance of texture and flavor is exactly right, food that looks and tastes delicious. And contrary to what many people believe, such foods do not have to include meat or fish, nor do they necessarily have to be elaborate.

I have collected here some of my favorite recipes, that can be served either for your own sheer indulgence or for those special occasions when gourmet food can contribute so much—occasions when you invite friends into your home, to enjoy good food and drink in a warm and relaxing atmosphere, when you linger over the table as the candles burn down and no one wants to move away. Or when you come home after some outdoor activity to delicious cooking smells and share a hearty meal in the kitchen, washed down with plenty of wine. Or special picnics in the country or by the sea. Or barbecues in the garden on long, warm summer evenings.

Food is at the heart of all these occasions, and with a little imagination you really can prepare wonderful vegetarian meals for them. But if you're vegetarian, or have vegetarian friends or relations to cook for, these meals can pose problems. What, for instance, can you grill at a barbecue? . . . And then there's that perennial question: What can you have instead of turkey for Christmas dinner?

And whereas meat eaters begin with the advantage of having something substantial, such as a turkey or a roast on which to base a meal, vegetarians have to make their meals from scratch, soaking dried beans and peas, chopping vegetables and grinding nuts, with no real tradition to guide them.

On the other hand this lack of convention can be an asset, because it frees you to experiment and invent new dishes, to try out different flavors and create interesting textures. It's enormously rewarding to surprise and delight people with a mouth-watering meal that doesn't contain any meat.

Cooking has become much easier and more fun now that so many exciting ingredients are readily available. I find much inspiration from looking around markets, specialty food shops and even my local supermarket, and seeing the luscious fruits and vegetables, wonderful cheeses, fragrant herbs and spices, all crying out to be tried. And once you start experimenting in the kitchen, it is amazing how one discovery leads to another and the ideas keep flowing.

All the recipes in this book, except for one or two classics such as the cheese fondue, are recipes I have devised for various occasions and tried out successfully on my family and friends. And although these dishes are delicious, nearly all of them are quite simple to make. For, while I love good food and enjoy making special meals, with three children— one not yet at school—I know very well what it is to have limited time and energy for cooking. So these recipes rely more on an imaginative use of good ingredients than on elaborate techniques. And, although undeniably more indulgent than some vegetarian dishes, they are still healthy and nutritional, being high in fiber and quite low in sugar and saturated fats. As for the cost, one of the many joys of vegetarian cooking is its economy. Some of the dishes, with their more exotic ingredients, are naturally more expensive to make, but they are easily compensated for by the savings made on meat and fish.

Surely one of the greatest satisfactions of life is to cook and serve a really delicious meal, a meal that nourishes the body and cheers the spirit, and may be remembered with pleasure for a long time to come. I hope that this book inspires many such delicious and happy occasions.

A Note on the American Edition

I just want to say how thrilled I am that this book is appearing in an American edition and to take this opportunity of saying hello from England. We have taken a great deal of care to convert the recipes to American measurements, pan sizes, and ingredients, and once again I should like to thank Lorraine Alexander Veach for her hard work and expertise here. I do hope that, as a result, you will find this a really useful book, and that you will enjoy its fare on many happy, festive occasions.

Rose Elliot, January 1983

The Festive Vegetarian

Cooking for Special Occasions

CHRISTMAS DINNER

As this is the one meal people always ask vegetarians about, perhaps I'd better begin here and reveal what vegetarians—this vegetarian, at any rate—eat for Christmas dinner.

This is a particularly difficult meal to plan because it is so strongly associated with the eating of turkey. People are much more conscious of not having turkey at a vegetarian Christmas dinner than they would be of not having meat at a dinner party, when they are not expecting any particular dish.

For this reason I am inclined to keep Christmas dinner as traditional as possible in other ways: I serve Brussels sprouts, chestnuts, roast potatoes, cranberry sauce and bread sauce, but with a savory nut loaf instead of turkey, followed by Christmas pudding and brandy or rum butter, or hard sauce. I find it difficult to resist changing the savory loaf in some way every year, but the one my family likes best is a pine-nut loaf with herb stuffing: the stuffing also provides another familiar Christmas flavor.

This is not a difficult meal to organize because the nut loaf can be made up to two days in advance and kept, well covered, in the fridge; or it can be stored in a freezer for up to two months. It will cook perfectly on the lower rack of quite a hot oven, with the potatoes roasting in their own pan above. The traditional dessert is, of course, usually made in advance, too; the brandy or rum butter can be made several days ahead and kept, again very well covered, in the fridge. It's always nice, too, to offer an alternative dessert the children will like, and ice cream is usually the most popular, but that too can be made beforehand.

This just leaves the first course. Usually, when planning a dinner party, for instance, I rather like to create an element of surprise—to produce something a bit unusual that startles people a little and makes them take notice of the food. But at Christmas I don't think it's worth it: there are just too many other distractions, and so a simple, refreshing fruity appetizer, to calm people down and get them ready for the rest of the meal, is best. My suggested menu is:

Pineapple Wedges
Pine-nut Loaf with Herb Stuffing
Special Wine Sauce · Bread Sauce · Apple and Cranberry Sauce
Roast Potatoes · Brussels Sprouts with Chestnuts
Christmas Pudding with Brandy Butter
and/or
Vanilla Ice Cream
with optional Hot Chestnut and Brandy Sauce

An alternative to the pine-nut loaf with herb stuffing would be the Chestnut, Sage and Red Wine Loaf (page 121), which brings to the meal the seasonal taste of chestnuts but in a slightly different form. My own favorite menu would revolve around the Walnut Pâté en Croûte, which is a moist, tasty nut loaf encased in golden flaky pastry. This would be best served with buttered baby new potatoes and brussels sprouts or with Purée of Brussels Sprouts, which cuts out the need for extra sauces.

Of course, there is a good deal more to Christmas cooking than this one meal, and it's helpful to have several other main dishes (and desserts, if possible) prepared and stored in the fridge or freezer, ready to be cooked when needed (see the section on informal lunch and supper parties, page 6).

DINNER PARTIES

A dinner party is more fun to plan than Christmas dinner because you have much greater freedom in the choice of dishes. I find six people, or at the most eight, is the right number for this kind of entertaining, and I usually plan a meal based on three or possibly four courses plus cheese. I certainly think it is helpful to make at least one of the courses, and preferably two, completely in advance. In fact, I am happiest with meals that require a minimum of attention at the time of the dinner party so that I can relax, knowing that everything is going to go smoothly.

It's very helpful to plan a first course that can already be in place when people come to the table—for example, any of the dips, with crudités or melba toast (which is easier than hot fingers of toast because it can be made in advance); artichokes served cold with a sour-cream filling; Surprise Avocados (page 43); or, for a summer dinner party when you want something spectacular, Grapefruit Rose Baskets (page 44). If, however, you don't mind doing a little last-minute preparation, Hot Avocado Tarts (page 56) make another mouth-watering and quite unusual appetizer, as do the little Mushroom Patties with Yoghurt and Scallion Sauce.

The final choice of appetizer will probably be governed by the main course you are serving; in fact, it's probably best to start by deciding on the main course and then to build the rest of the meal around that.

An easy way of producing a comparatively conventional main course is to choose a savory loaf, as for Christmas dinner, with accompanying sauces and cooked vegetables. The Walnut Pâté en Croûte, Flaky Mushroom Roll and, in the summer, Stuffed Zucchini Baked with Butter and Thyme are possibilities. As they are all quite rich, I would be inclined to serve them with fairly simply cooked vegetables.

The dessert can certainly be made beforehand because there are so many delicious cold ones to choose from. Sherbet is always good after a rich meal, especially if it can be served in an interesting way. The two-color Melon Sherbet with Crystallized Mint Leaves is lovely, as is the Rose Sherbet, because of its unusual perfumed flavor. Don't forget to take these out of the freezer at least an hour before you want to serve them.

Fruit desserts are refreshing after a rich meal. Sweet pastry dishes are also very popular and, if I can, I usually offer one as an alternative to the lighter desserts.

Most people like some cheese at the end of the meal, either before or after the dessert course, and here it's probably best to offer one or at most two really good cheeses, such as a perfect wedge of Brie and a piece of properly matured Cheddar, followed by plenty of good coffee, black or with cream.

Here are some suggested menus:

Artichokes with Sour-Cream Filling
Walnut Pâté en Croûte
New Potatoes with Butter and Parsley
Purée of Brussels Sprouts or Ratatouille
Green Herb Salad
Stuffed Pineapple Halves

Striped Pâté with Melba Toast
Flaky Mushroom Roll with Yoghurt and Scallion Sauce
Endive and Walnut Salad
Strawberry Cheesecake or Special Fruit Salad

Grapefruit Rose Baskets
Stuffed Zucchini Baked with Butter and Thyme
Potato and Turnip Purée · Buttered Baby Carrots
Cabbage Salad
Jeweled Fruit Flan or Raspberry Ice Cream

Hot Avocado Tarts
Spinach Roulade · Lemon Potatoes
Braised Cucumber with Walnuts
Peaches in Strawberry Purée with Crisp Biscuits

Bean and Ripe Olive Pâté with Melba Toast
Hot Avocado with Wine Stuffing
Potato Purée with Cream, Butter and lots of Black Pepper
Chinese Cabbage with Scallions · Oven-Baked Carrots
Black-Currant Lattice with Lemon Pastry Tart

INFORMAL LUNCHES AND SUPPERS

For this kind of easy-going entertaining, when you invite a group of people for supper or Sunday brunch, you can either eat in the kitchen or let people serve themselves from dishes laid out buffet style, standing and chatting as they eat or sitting where best they can.

I don't think an appetizer is necessarily called for, though one or two different dips with lots of crudités or melba toast is an easy and always colorful beginning to any meal. If it's a cold day, hot soup and rolls or garlic bread might be preferable.

For the main course I go for dishes that don't need fiddly sauces and accompaniments, and can be served with just a good green salad. Favorites are pizza, which is always a success, rice dishes, lasagne, or stuffed crêpes. Quiche or vegetable pie is also very good for this kind of entertaining.

It's a good idea to offer a choice of desserts. If the party is at lunchtime and includes children, I would be inclined to offer homemade vanilla ice cream as one possibility because this is something that most of them are sure to like. To go with this, I would suggest a fruit dessert along with something a bit more substantial, such as one of the cheesecakes. For a real celebration, Raspberry Meringue Gâteau is always a treat.

Some suggested menus might be:

Tomato and Fresh Basil Soup with Cream and Garlic Bread
Eggplant, Red Pepper and Cheese Quiche
New Potatoes · Chunky Mixed Salad Bowl
Chestnut Ice Cream

Melon Halves with Strawberries
Special Pizza · Green Herb Salad
Almond and Chocolate Flan
or Raspberry Meringue Gâteau

Carrot, Apple and Chervil Soup with Warm Whole-Wheat Rolls
Lentil Lasagne
Green Herb Salad
Special Fruit Salad
Strawberry Cheesecake

Cheddar Cheese and Red Wine Dip
with Melba Toast and Crudités
Mushroom Rice with Almonds and Red Pepper
Chunky Mixed Salad Bowl
Pears in Cider with Ginger · Vanilla Ice Cream

I am thinking here of those occasions when you go out with family and friends, perhaps for a Sunday walk, and want to come back to the delicious aroma of something cooking in the oven. Or those times when you've been out to some evening function and you want to come back and find a meal all ready, or one needing only a minimum of attention.

Three such dishes are: Lima Bean and Cider Casserole, which, if you add potatoes, only needs a crisp, refreshing salad to go with it; Deep-Dish Vegetable Pie, delicious with a cold, creamy, sharp-tasting sauce and a green salad; and Mushroom Pudding, which will steam gently away in the oven if you set it in a large casserole or roasting pan containing boiling water and put some foil over the top. Red Cabbage with Apples Baked in Cider can cook in the oven beside the Mushroom Pudding, and the two together make a lovely filling meal to come home to on a chilly day. You could even put a Spiced Plum Crumble in the oven at the same time if it's going to be a very long walk and there are hearty appetites among those in the party! Alternatively, if you prefer something lighter, I suggest one of the cold fruit desserts that can both be left ready.

Suggested menus would be:

Lima Bean and Cider Casserole
Onion Rice
Green Herb Salad
Biscuits and Cheese

Mushroom Pudding
Red Cabbage with Apples Baked in Cider
Baked Potatoes with Sour Cream
Spiced Plum Crumble or *Kiwi Fruit in Grape Gelatin*

When you want to come home to a meal in the evening perhaps something a little more elegant is called for. You might want to start with crudités, which people can start nibbling while you do anything that's necessary for the main course, or a hot bowl of soup. For the main course you could serve a choice of two or more different cold savories and bowls of different colored salads to go with them. Choose salads that can be covered with plastic wrap and left without spoiling while you are out. This can be followed by a good cheese board and a light dessert.

These meals might shape up like this:

Cheddar Cheese and Red Wine Dip with Crudités
Cold Lentil, Hazelnut and Cider Loaf · Mayonnaise
Asparagus Quiche
Potato Salad · Tomato and Lima Beans with Basil Dressing
Jeweled Fruit Tart

Celery Soup with Warm Rolls
Molded Rice and Artichoke-Heart Salad
White Nut Loaf with Capers · Mayonnaise
Cabbage Salad with Nuts and Raisins
Lima Bean, Tomato and Olive Salad
Apple Salad
Strawberry Cheesecake

IMPROMPTU MEALS FOR TWO

I have to admit that making a special meal on the spur of the moment is quite difficult for vegetarians: most of our food does take a certain amount of preparation and there are very few gourmet ready-made foods we can fall back on. Luckily, however, we can rely heavily on fresh fruits and raw vegetables.

Choose a first course that requires little or no actual cooking, just assembling. If you keep a good vinaigrette on hand in the fridge—such as the one for Surprise Avocados (page 43)—then you have merely to settle on a vegetable that can be served raw or barely steamed with that dressing. Or you may choose a combination of fresh fruits to begin your meal. Or crudités served with one or several of the dip recipes.

Provided the circumstances of this impromptu meal allow you to do some preliminary shopping, a meal that's really quick to prepare consists of a good bread, perhaps two kinds; several interesting cheeses; and a large mixed salad as the main course. Although it's simple, this makes a surprisingly satisfactory feast served with chilled white wine, plenty of fresh fruit for dessert and coffee.

If you stick to a simple first course and make your salad an accompaniment rather than a main course, you may prefer to build your meal around Cheese Fondue, my very favorite wintertime main course particularly when you are only two for dinner. Serve a nice wine and finish with fresh fruit and coffee, and you'll find you've produced a very pleasant, simple, and yet quite elegant meal.

Pasta and omelettes are further possibilities. Add to the basic ingredients some fresh or dried herbs, onion if you like, butter or oil (olive or walnut), and grated cheese, and you're set. A crunchy green salad goes well with this, as does a good bought ice cream for dessert.

It's a good idea to keep one or two cans of interesting vegetables in the cupboard for these occasions. Useful ones include artichoke hearts, tomatoes, red kidney beans, and chick peas. Nuts, another key ingredient, should also be on hand.

Among the countless menus it is possible to create using only these basic guidelines, I suggest:

Quick Hummus with Crudités
Spaghetti with Tomato Sauce · Garlic Bread
Green Herb Salad
Pineapple Wedges and Vanilla Ice Cream

Surprise Avocados
Cheese Fondue with Whole-Wheat Fingers
Tomato and Lima Bean Salad with Basil Dressing
Half Melons with Strawberries

Chunky Mixed Salad Bowl
Choice of Breads and Cheeses
Fresh Mangoes

OUTDOOR EATING: BARBECUES AND PICNICS

Barbecues are fun in the summer, but for vegetarians a little planning and preparation is necessary as the sausages or burgers for grilling have to be made first from nuts or lentils! The Lentil and Mushroom Burgers work very well and are delicious served with hot rolls or French bread and mustard or chutney. An alternative is to make a savory loaf and cut that up and grill it: the Lentil and Cider Loaf can be treated in this way because it slices particularly well.

Hot baked potatoes filled with sour cream are delicious eaten out of doors, but don't rely on the barbecue to cook them; I think it is much more satisfactory to do them in the oven, then wrap them in foil and just keep them warm with whatever cooking facilities are available outside. To go with these you need lots of good salad: the Chunky Mixed Salad Bowl is ideal, or my favorite well-dressed Green Herb Salad, which I am afraid seems to crop up at nearly every meal.

I don't think an appetizer is necessary for a barbecue, though you could nibble crudités with a dip while the food is cooking. But you do need lots of food and plenty to drink: chilled cider, lager or beer, and some fairly substantial desserts such as Bakewell Tart or a good cake seem to go down well.

Here is a suggested menu:

Crudités and Cheddar Cheese with Red Wine
Baked Potatoes with Sour Cream
Lentil and Mushroom Burgers with Mustard, Chutney and
Soft Rolls
Chunky Mixed Salad Bowl
Fresh Summer Fruits
Candied Peel, Ginger and Almond Cake

When it comes to special picnics, I think it adds to the occasion if you do begin with an appetizer. Chilled soup would be very pleasant. Or you could always take hot soup in a Thermos, if, when the day arrives, it looks as though the weather is going to be bad. Otherwise, you could serve fruit prepared at home and put together again for transporting, or a tangy dip with crudités.

The main course has to be based on salad which can be kept crisp in an insulated container or, not very elegant but effective, can be transported in a large saucepan with a close-fitting lid and transferred to a bowl for serving. To go with this I suggest a cold savory loaf. Any sauce you choose must keep well unrefrigerated.

One of my favorite desserts for a summer picnic is strawberries and cream, but the cream might spoil, and a cake or tart of some kind is also usually appreciated since everyone always seems to eat more in the fresh air. To go with a picnic, have a wine that's fun and easy to drink, like a sparkling rosé, or some beer and lemonade for the thirsty ones.

A good menu for a special picnic would be:

Chilled Raspberry and Cranberry Soup
Apple Salad
Chunky Mixed Salad Bowl
Soft Whole-Wheat Rolls
Candied Peel, Ginger, and Almond Cake
Vanilla Drops

COCKTAIL PARTIES, BUFFETS, RECEPTIONS

For a cocktail party, you just want tasty nibbles—food that's attractive to look at and easy to eat when you're trying to balance a drink and chat at the same time under somewhat noisy and crowded conditions. It's best if most of the food can be prepared in advance, though it is nice to be able to bring out one or two hot savories halfway through if you can.

Suggested food might be:

Asparagus Rolls · Colored Pinwheels
Miniature Open Sandwiches · Baby Scones
Mushroom Patties
Whole-Wheat Cheese Straws
Miniature Curried Lentil Rissoles with
Yoghurt and Sour-Cream Sauce

The pastry dishes would be delightful served hot from the oven if you could manage it, but they would also be all right cold. Hot or cold, the portions should be small.

For a buffet, or something like a wedding reception or christening party, you usually need food that's more substantial and can be eaten easily with a fork. Perhaps the main headache here is how much to prepare. Quantities are difficult to judge; when people are together at these occasions, they tend to eat less than you think they will.

My own rough-and-ready way of working out quantities is to think what I would eat myself and multiply it by the number of people who are going to be present! This simple method works very well; remember that if you offer a variety of salads and savories people will probably have tiny helpings of lots of different things, to try as many as possible. Here is a sample menu:

Vegetarian Scotch Eggs
Deep-Dish Mushroom Pie
White Nut Loaf with Capers
Lemon Mayonnaise or Yoghurt and Herb Sauce
Molded Rice and Artichoke-Heart Salad
Potato Salad
Red Kidney Bean, Carrot and Walnut Salad
Stilton Log with Pears
Apricot Gelatin with Fresh Apricots and Strawberries
Crunchy Ginger Cookies
Vanilla Drops
Chocolate Hazelnut Gâteau

Wine with Vegetarian Food

WHEN choosing wine, the same principles apply for a vegetarian meal as for any other type of meal: you need wine with the right amount of weight and body for the kind of food you're serving, and you should choose something you like. There is, of course, no tradition for what you should or should not drink with a nut loaf, and, if you have a favorite recipe, you might want to experiment by serving it with different wines on various occasions to see which you prefer.

Here are a few suggestions that I hope might be helpful as a general guide.

BEFORE THE MEAL

The ideal aperitif is fresh-tasting, even slightly astringent, to stimulate the appetite and wake up the palate in preparation for the food to come. Most people have their own particular favorite, but a popular alternative to the usual drinks is a crisp dry wine, such as a Chablis, Mâcon Villages or Muscadet from France, a Soave or Frascati from Italy, Dão from Portugal or the spicy German Gewürztraminer, to mention just a few. A pleasant variation is to add a few drops of black-currant liqueur, cassis, to the wine to make the pretty pink drink, Kir. The proportions are five of wine to one of cassis, and traditionally the wine should be Aligoté, but any dry, crisp, inexpensive white wine will do.

These wines should of course be well chilled, and, if you serve sherry, that too should be chilled. It is surprising what a difference this makes: a chilled dry fino sherry or the slightly salty-tasting Manzanilla are hard to beat, though many people prefer a medium-dry sherry and you should offer this as an alternative, especially if you are planning to start the meal with a mellow fruit dish, such as melon or pineapple.

Chilled dry white vermouth, especially the French Chambéry, is also very pleasant served with ice and a slice of lemon or topped with tonic water or equal quantities of apple and orange juice and a sprig of mint—particularly refreshing to drink in the garden on a warm summer evening.

WITH THE FIRST COURSE

Having specific wines to go with the different courses of a meal creates a feeling of luxury and celebration. And it's not that extravagant if you are going to need two bottles of wine anyway for a dinner party of, say, six people. The basic rule here is dry before sweet and youth before age. Be careful, too, about serving white wines after red. This doesn't apply to the glorious, honeyed-sweet white dessert wine with which you might wish to round off the meal; but don't serve an ordinary dry or medium-dry white wine after a full, rounded red; the white will seem poor by comparison. If in doubt, taste the wines beforehand to check whether they will follow each other well: you only have to try a dry wine after a sweet one, or an inexpensive immature one after a good one, to realize the reason for this rule; there are occasions when it can be broken with aplomb, but you need to know your wines well in order to do so.

Generally speaking, soups do not go particularly well with wine, neither do dishes with sharp-tasting vinaigrette dressings, nor tart fruits, such as grapefruit. On the other hand, sweet pineapple and melon are pleasant with a medium-dry sherry, perhaps carried over from the pre-meal drinks.

Creamy first courses, such as the Artichokes with Sour-Cream Filling, Surprise Avocados, Striped Pâté and Sour-Cream Dip with Crudités need a fairly full-bodied, dry white wine of the type you might serve with fish. The wines I have suggested as aperitifs would actually do very well and could be carried through to the meal. I also like an aperitif drink, Manzanilla sherry, with the tangy Bean and Ripe Olive Pâté and with hummus. It is, in fact, a good idea to bear in mind what you are going to have for the first course of the meal when offering the drinks beforehand.

With the Cheddar Cheese and Red Wine Dip and the Stilton Log with Pears, you might try an Italian Barbera for the former (you could use some to make the dip, too) and a port, perhaps a Portugese white or a tawny, for the Stilton.

The various patties and pastries would be enhanced by a dry white wine but the Curried Vegetable and Nut Pâté, and the Miniature Curried Lentil Rissoles are probably better without.

WITH THE MAIN COURSE

The rich Asparagus in Hot Lemon Mayonnaise and Salsify with White Wine and Mushrooms need a dry, full-bodied white wine or a really dry rosé to stand up to them—and I would treat the Spinach Roulade in the same way. Vouvray, Chablis, Sylvaner, Soave, Riesling and Gewürtztraminer are possibilities.

When it comes to the Stuffed Red Peppers with Almonds, the Tomatoes Stuffed with Pine Nuts and the Hot Avocado with Wine Stuffing, which are all strongly flavored with either tomatoes or herbs, I would suggest a full-bodied wine from an area where these ingredients are used in the local cuisine. A Côtes de Provence would do very well. The rich Stuffed Zucchini Baked with Butter and Thyme also needs a robust wine to go with it: you could serve a full-bodied white, but I think a red, such as a Burgundy, Bordeaux or Rhône would be a better choice, or a Spanish Rioja.

As for the pastry dishes, dry or medium-dry white wine would go well with the Asparagus Quiche; a red or a full-bodied white wine with the Eggplant, Red Pepper and Cheese Quiche, while the Walnut Pâté en Croûte needs a Burgundy or claret. I think I'd choose an Italian red, perhaps the Barbera again, to go with the Cauliflower, Stilton and Walnut Quiche, which is strongly flavored.

Italian red wine, perhaps a Chianti or Barbera, would also be my first choice for the Italian-style dishes—Special Pizza, Lentil Lasagne and Spaghetti with Lentil and Wine Sauce. A Californian red, made from the Zinfandel grape, also goes well with these, while for the Baked Crêpes with Leeks either a white or red, again with some body. For the Mushroom Rice with Almonds and Red Pepper, I would try a Spanish wine, either a full-bodied white or a red. Strictly speaking, I suppose Cheese Fondue should be served with a dry Swiss wine but I would suggest any good dry or medium-dry white, perhaps a Soave.

Rather as with chicken and turkey, you could serve either a white or a red wine with the nut loaves, though I think the Chestnut, Sage and Red Wine Loaf, the White Nut Loaf with Capers and the Pine Nut Loaf with its herb stuffing, on the whole go best with red, since they are all fairly highly flavored. A claret or its equivalent would do very nicely.

These nut loaves and also the Walnut Pâté en Croûte all slice well when they're cold; try them with an assortment of pretty salads and some chilled dry or medium-dry white or rosé wine, or a red for the walnut pâté, perhaps a chilled Beaujolais for a change. And for a summer picnic, something that's light and easy to drink like a Rhine wine, perhaps the delicate, flowery Piesporter or, for fun, one of the many good sparkling wines that are now available, either white or rosé.

WITH THE CHEESE AND DESSERT

Wine connoisseurs suggest serving the cheese before the dessert so that you can finish off the last of the red wine with the cheese before moving on to the dessert and the sweet wine; or you could have the dessert and then some cheese with port. It is certainly a treat to round off a special meal with a really glorious, sweet wine, but I personally prefer to enjoy these on their own, or perhaps with a perfectly ripe, fragrant melon, a simple fresh fruit salad, Stuffed Pineapple Halves or Peaches in Strawberry Purée.

Vegetarian Nutrition

Although nutrition may not be the main thing on your mind when you're cooking for a special occasion, if you're planning meals that exclude meat and fish, it's helpful to know a few facts about protein.

Protein in a vegetarian diet comes mainly from four groups of foods:

Dairy: eggs, milk and milk products, such as cheese and yoghurt;

Nuts and Seeds: all kinds of nuts, also sunflower and sesame seeds, which are excellent sources of protein. Peanuts actually belong to the dried bean group, though they are rich in protein, while chestnuts are a carbohydrate food and are not a good source;

Dried beans: the large group of dried lentils, peas and beans, all of which contain valuable amounts of protein;

Grains: including breads, cereals, rice, and pasta. Although often considered merely as carbohydrate foods, grains do in fact contain some protein: three slices of bread, for instance, supply nearly a third of the daily protein requirement of an average man.

Daily protein requirement figures are revised from time to time as our understanding of nutrition increases. In England, it is interesting to note, the amount of protein recommended now is half what it was in 1948. The latest figures, published in England by the Department of Health and Social Security in 1969, suggest a daily intake of 1.7 grams of protein for every kilogram (2.2 pounds) of body weight for a child, and 0.59 grams per kilo of body weight for an adult. (Adults require less protein than do growing adolescents, since adults use their protein mainly for repair of tissues, not for growth.)

American nutritional figures differ slightly, recommending that an adult male take in 56 grams of protein each day (although this amount can vary depending on age, body weight, and general health).

The following table shows the amount of protein that can be provided by a variety of vegetarian foods:

Food	Grams of Protein per Cup
whole-wheat bread	3.0 (per slice)
macaroni (cooked)	5.3
flour, whole-wheat	16.0
rice (cooked)	4.0
soy flour (full fat)	26.4
Shredded Wheat	3.5
cheese, Cheddar, grated	28.0
cheese, cottage, creamed	33.3
cheese, Parmesan	12.0 (per ounce)
milk, whole	8.4
eggs, 1 whole	6.4
lima beans (cooked)	13.0
lentils, dried (cooked)	15.8
almonds	26.0
Brazil nuts	20.0
chestnuts	3.3 (4 ounces)
peanuts (roasted and salted)	37.0
walnuts (chopped)	17.8
potatoes (baked)	3.0
cabbage, raw (shredded)	0.9

From this it is easy to see that the average protein requirement of 56 grams can be met by having, say:

2 slices whole-wheat bread	6.0 grams
1 cup whole milk	8.4

(Information on protein requirement: Food and Nutrition Board, National Academy of Science and National Research Council, Washington, D.C., 2101 Constitution Avenue 20418.)

1 medium baked potato	3.0
½ cup cottage cheese	16.5
1 egg	6.4
1 cup lentils	15.8

Another point that concerns some people is whether the quality of protein obtained from vegetarian sources is as good as that derived from meat and fish.

The fact is that all protein is made up of about twenty-two different amino acids that are present in different foods in various quantities and combinations. Of these amino acids there are eight that are said to be "essential" amino acids because the body cannot synthesize them. These essential amino acids all have to be present at the same time and, if the body is going to use them most economically, in the right proportions. This means that, if a food only contains half the necessary amount of one of these essential amino acids, the body can use only half of each of the others, wasting the rest.

The proportions of essential amino acids found in animal proteins, including eggs, are close to the requirements of the body. Most vegetable protein is, on the other hand, short on one or two of the essential amino acids, which means that not all their protein can be utilized.

The good news, though, is that the different groups of proteins— dairy, nuts and seeds, dried beans and grains—are deficient in *different* essential amino acids. So, if you mix the protein from two or more groups at the same meal, you end up with more available protein than would otherwise be the case—up to about fifty percent in some instances. Thus, if you mix your proteins (as frequently happens naturally at a meal anyway), it's actually easier to reach the recommended protein levels on a vegetarian diet.

As far as the planning of individual meals is concerned, it is a good idea to think of the protein the meal as a whole offers, and if the main course happens to be a vegetable or grain-based one, make up for any possible deficiency by serving a protein-rich appetizer or dessert to round off the meal. In this book, most of the main course dishes are in fact rich in protein, and, in the few cases where this is not so, I have made suggestions within the recipe for increasing the protein content of the meal.

A Note on Ingredients

Most of the ingredients in this book are readily available, but here are a few notes that might be helpful.

DAIRY PRODUCTS

Cheese: is an excellent source of protein and an extremely versatile food. You should be very aware, however, that cheeses can vary widely in the amount of fat they contain, and in the amount of salt. (See the table on cheeses, page 22.) Hard cheeses tend to contain less fat than soft, runny cheeses. Parmesan is very high in salt, but is usually grated and used in small quantities as a garnish or for its pungent flavor. The best way to educate yourself about which cheeses best satisfy your individual nutritional needs is to ask your grocer or cheese-shop clerk; the proprietors of the smaller specialty shops are often more knowledgeable than the managers or clerks in big grocery chains, but the only way to discover who your best sources of information are is to ask. Some cheeses carry the necessary information on their labels, of course.

Most *hard cheeses* contain rennet, a substance generally taken from the stomach of calves. Some vegetarians may find this objectionable, and if so there are viable alternatives. Most health-food shops do stock cheeses made with non-animal rennet; many kosher cheeses, too, are marked to indicate whether they contain animal or non-animal rennet.

Among the most versatile cheeses for cooking purposes are *cottage* and *ricotta*. They are fairly low in fat (ricotta can be bought in whole-milk and part-skim-milk varieties) and are good binders in the preparation of many vegetarian dishes. In addition to cheeses, *sour cream* and *yoghurt* are also widely used, and can be combined with ricotta, cottage cheese, and a large range of seasonings in loaves, quiches, sauces and dips.

Cheese	*Calories*	*Protein (g)*	*Fat (g)*
Cheddar (1 ounce)	114	7.06	9.40
Cottage, Creamed 4% (1 cup)	217	26.23	9.47
Lowfat 2% (1 cup)	203	31.05	4.36
Lowfat 1% (1 cup)	164	28.00	2.30
Cream (1 ounce)	99	2.14	9.89
Parmesan, Grated (1 ounce)	129	11.78	8.51
Hard (1 ounce)	111	10.14	7.32
Ricotta, Whole Milk (1 cup)	428	27.70	31.93
Partially Skim (1 cup)	340	28.02	19.46

* Source: Dairy Council Digest.

Butter and margarine: I use both butter and margarine in cooking but try to do so sparingly, reserving butter for those dishes that really need its special flavor and only buying a margarine high in poly-unsaturated fats.

NUTS

Although nuts are expensive, they compare favorably with meat when you consider the quantities used. In this book I have used mainly cashew nuts, almonds—blanched and ground for "white" dishes and with the skins on for "brown" dishes—and pine nuts for the occasional treat, as well as Brazil nuts, peanuts, walnuts, which I love as long as they are fresh, and hazelnuts (greatly improved if lightly roasted before use). To do this, simply spread the nuts out on a baking sheet and bake in a moderate oven for about 20 minutes, until the nuts underneath the brown outer skin are golden brown. You can rub off the outer skins, if you like, but I don't bother normally. Unsalted peanuts can be treated similarly. All these nuts can be quickly ground in a blender or food processor.

DRIED BEANS AND PEAS

Lima beans, chick peas, red kidney beans, and lentils are all used in the recipes in this book. All benefit from being soaked before cooking. They can either be covered with cold water and left for several hours or boiled for 2–3 minutes and then left to soak in the hot water for 1 hour: both methods work well, and it's good idea to drain the beans in a colander and rinse them before covering them with fresh cold water and simmering them until tender. The rinsing helps to make them more digestible.

FATS

Apart from butter and margarine (see under Dairy Products), I use a polyunsaturated vegetable oil for cooking—either soya, which is a good healthy general-purpose oil, or sunflower, which has a pleasant lightness making it more suitable for some dishes. For salads there is nothing to beat best-quality olive oil, with some walnut or (if you can get it) hazelnut oil added sometimes as a special treat.

FLOUR

I have used whole-wheat flour in the majority of recipes but I recommend a mixture of whole-wheat flour and unbleached for flaky pastry and for some of the cakes and cookies.

SUGAR

I am firmly of the opinion that sugar should be given only a very limited place in our diets, but I have used it for some of the desserts intended as treats rather than for everyday eating. For many of these it's very useful to have some vanilla sugar handy, and all you need do to make this is break a vanilla bean in half and bury it in a jar of superfine or confectioners sugar, adding more sugar as it is used.

Although vegetarian stock cubes are available in health-food shops and supermarkets, nothing can replace the delicate flavor of a good homemade stock. Vegetable stock is easy to make (see page 29) and you can make enough for several days at a time and keep it in a covered jar in the refrigerator.

It's surprising, too, what a difference the addition of a glassful of wine or vermouth can make to an ordinary dish, giving it a richness that makes the final seasoning so much simpler. If I am buying wine for a special meal and I just need a little for the cooking, then I use that; otherwise I buy something cheaper, but not too acid or too sweet. For some dishes it's useful to have some fino sherry or a dry, sherry-type wine. Small quantities of brandy and liqueurs are used in a few of the recipes.

For sauces and salad dressings, nothing can beat a good wine vinegar—I like red wine vinegar best—but for a change you might like to try raspberry vinegar, if you can get it, for a pleasant fruity flavor.

FLAVORINGS

Fresh herbs are of course best, though not always available. I find bags of bouquet garnis useful, also dried thyme, basil and oregano. Of the fresh herbs, definitely parsley and chives, and as many of the following as possible: basil, tarragon, chervil, mint, thyme and fennel.

I also use a good deal of *garlic*, which I think helps to make vegetarian food tasty; I especially like those lovely strings of fat, juicy garlic from France.

Sea salt is easy to get now and fine enough to use without a grinder. It's healthiest to under- rather than over-salt dishes and let people add more at the table if necessary.

I like *freshly ground black pepper* from a pepper mill, but I also very much like the flavor of a coarsely ground bottled lemon pepper.

Of the *spices*, nutmeg, grated on a small grater as you need it, and powdered mace are the most useful. I also like curry powder, coriander (whole and ground), ground cumin and turmeric. Mustard is indispensable, and I like to have three types available if possible: dry mustard and two prepared ones: a mild, whole-grain type that is lovely for adding to salad dressings and for serving with nut burgers and loaves, and Dijon-style, which is good in sauces. Tabasco sauce is ideal for adding bite to dips and cheese dishes.

JELLING AGENTS

Instead of gelatin, which is unsuitable for strict vegetarians because it's made from the bones and hooves of animals, I use agar agar. This is a fine powder made from seaweed and, in my opinion, the best of the vegetarian jelling agents and very easy to use: you just beat the agar agar into the boiling liquid, a teaspoon for each 1¼ cups of liquid, then let it boil for 1 minute.

Soups

Vegetarian Stock

Jerusalem Artichoke Soup

Carrot, Apple and Chervil Soup

Cauliflower Soup with Almonds

Celery Soup

Green Pea Soup with Mint and Cream

Chilled Raspberry and Cranberry Soup

Tomato and Fresh Basil Soup with Cream

$\mathcal{S}$oup makes an excellent hot first course. It's simple to prepare and requires very little last-minute attention, yet I have found that it's always greatly appreciated and people think you've gone to a great deal more trouble than you have.

Part of the secret lies in presenting the soup attractively: A swirl of cream and some chopped fresh basil make a simple homemade tomato soup look and taste special; some cream and chopped mint add the finishing touch to a smooth green pea soup, while a delicately flavored white soup, like creamy cauliflower or artichoke, is delicious with chopped chives, crunchy golden croutons or nuts on top.

All the vegetable soups in this section freeze well, but I wouldn't try to freeze the chilled raspberry one: it's better to freeze the raspberries and then make the soup quickly when you need it.

VEGETARIAN STOCK

Although you can now buy vegetarian stock cubes, homemade stock is so much better and it is very easy to make. It only takes about 10 minutes to prepare (followed by 1 hour slow simmering) and it keeps perfectly for a week in a jar in the bottom of the refrigerator. You can add some garlic, peppercorns and other herbs, such as a bay leaf and some thyme, but this is a good basic recipe that works well for most purposes. *Makes about 4 cups.*

1 onion, peeled and roughly sliced	1 medium-size potato, scrubbed
1 stalk of celery, washed and	and roughly chopped
roughly chopped	2 or 3 sprigs of parsley
1 large carrot, scrubbed and	2½ quarts water
roughly chopped	

Put the vegetables and parsley into a large saucepan and add the water. Bring to the boil, then turn the heat down, cover and leave to simmer for 1 hour. Strain and serve.

JERUSALEM ARTICHOKE SOUP

Jerusalem artichokes make a beautiful creamy white soup with a delicate flavor I think is delicious. They are quite easy to peel if you use a potato peeler and are fairly ruthless about cutting off the little lumps. Put them into a bowl of cold water as they're done, to preserve their color. *Serves 6.*

2 tablespoons butter or	1¼ cups milk
polyunsaturated margarine	⅔ cup light cream—optional
1 onion, peeled and chopped	Sea salt
2 pounds Jerusalem artichokes,	Freshly ground black pepper
peeled and cut into even-sized	Nutmeg, freshly grated
chunks	Fresh chives or parsley, chopped
4½ cups light vegetable stock or	
water	

Melt the butter in a large saucepan and add the onion; sauté for 5–7 minutes until fairly soft but not browned, then put in the artichoke and cook for a further 2–3 minutes, stirring often. Pour in the stock or water and bring up to the boil, then turn the heat down, put a lid on the saucepan and leave to simmer for about 20 minutes until the artichoke is soft. Purée in a blender or food processor, then add enough of the milk to bring the soup to the right consistency, together with the cream if you're using it. Season with salt, pepper and freshly grated nutmeg to taste. Reheat, and serve with chopped chives or parsley sprinkled on top.

CARROT, APPLE AND CHERVIL SOUP

Feathery leaves of chervil have a beautifully delicate flavor I think makes this soup special. But if you can't get chervil you can use other fresh herbs instead: tarragon or fennel would be good. This soup is also good chilled. *Serves 4–6.*

2 tablespoons butter or
  polyunsaturated margarine—
  or 2 tabespoons oil if you're
  planning to serve it chilled
1 onion, peeled and chopped
½ pound carrots, scraped and
  sliced
1 cooking apple, peeled, cored
  and sliced

1 stalk celery, washed and sliced
4½ cups light vegetable stock or
  water
Sea salt
Freshly ground black pepper
Sugar
2 tablespoons chopped fresh
  chervil

Melt the butter in a large saucepan and add the onion; sauté for 5–7 minutes until fairly soft but not browned, then put in the carrot, apple and celery and cook for a further 2–3 minutes, stirring often. Pour in the stock or water and bring up to the boil, then turn the heat down, put a lid on the saucepan and leave to simmer for about 20 minutes, until the carrots are soft. Purée in a blender or food processor, and add a little extra stock if necessary to make a fairly thin, creamy consistency. Season with salt, pepper and perhaps just a touch of sugar.

Reheat, and serve each bowl with a good sprinkling of chopped chervil on top—the bright green looks very pretty against the orange soup.

CAULIFLOWER SOUP WITH ALMONDS

Cauliflower makes a surprisingly satisfactory soup, creamy and delicately flavored. It goes very well with the herb bread on page 195, but if you haven't time to make this, hot garlic bread is also good. Prepare this in the usual way by making diagonal cuts in a French loaf, not quite through the bottom crust, spreading the cut surfaces generously with a mixture of butter and crushed garlic, then wrapping the loaf in foil and baking in a hot oven for 15–20 minutes, until the crust is crisp and the inside deliciously hot and buttery. *Serves 6.*

2 tablespoons butter or
   polyunsaturated margarine
1 onion, peeled and chopped
1 medium-size potato, peeled
   and chopped
½ fairly small cauliflower, washed
   and broken into florets
4½ cups light vegetable stock or
   water

Sea salt
Freshly ground black pepper
Nutmeg
⅔ cup light cream—optional
2 tablespoons slivered roasted
   almonds

Melt the butter in a large saucepan and add the onion; sauté for 5–7 minutes until fairly soft but not browned, then put in the potato and cauliflower and cook for a further 2–3 minutes, stirring often: the vegetables for this soup mustn't brown or the delicate flavor will be spoilt. Pour in the stock or water and bring up to the boil, then turn the heat down, put a lid on the saucepan and leave to simmer for about 20 minutes, until the vegetables are soft. Purée in a blender or food processor, then add the cream, if you're using it, and season well with salt and plenty of freshly grated pepper and nutmeg. Reheat, and serve with crisp slivered almonds on top of each portion.

CELERY SOUP

This is an economical soup because you can use the outside stalks of celery, saving the hearts for a salad. Some tender leaves from the celery, chopped or snipped with kitchen scissors, make an attractive garnish. *Serves 6.*

2 tablespoons butter or
   polyunsaturated margarine
1 onion, peeled and chopped
Outside stalks from 1 head of
   celery—about 1 pound—
   washed and sliced
½ pound potatoes, peeled and cut
   into even-size chunks

4½ cups light vegetable stock or
   water
2 tablespoons chopped fresh
   celery leaves
⅔ cup light cream—optional
Sea salt
Freshly ground black pepper

Melt the butter in a large saucepan and add the onion; fry for 5–7 minutes until fairly soft but not browned, then put in the celery and potato and cook for a further 2–3 minutes, stirring often. Pour in the stock or water and bring up to the boil, then turn the heat down, put a lid on the saucepan and leave to simmer for about 20 minutes until the vegetables are soft. Purée the mixture in a blender or food processor, then add the celery leaves, the cream if you're using it, and a good seasoning of salt and pepper. Reheat before serving. Or serve each bowlful with a swirl of cream and some chopped celery leaves on top.

GREEN PEA SOUP WITH MINT AND CREAM

Frozen peas make a beautiful vivid green soup with a very smooth texture. It looks lovely swirled with cream and flecked with dark green chopped mint, and is good either hot or chilled. *Serves 6.*

2 tablespoons butter or
   polyunsaturated margarine—or
   2 tablespoons oil if you're
   planning to serve it chilled
1 onion, peeled and chopped
2 pounds frozen peas
4½ cups light vegetable stock or
   water

A few sprigs of thyme, if available
Sea salt
Freshly ground black pepper
⅔ cup light cream—optional
2 tablespoons chopped fresh mint

Melt the butter in a large saucepan and add the onion; sauté for 5–7 minutes until fairly soft but not browned, then add the peas and cook for a further 2–3 minutes, stirring often. Pour in the stock or water, add the thyme, and bring mixture up to the boil; then turn the heat down, put a lid on the saucepan and leave to simmer for about 20 minutes until the vegetables are soft. Purée, then sieve, pushing through as much of the pea purée as you can. Pour the soup back into the saucepan and season carefully with salt and pepper. Reheat, then serve in bowls, garnishing with a spoonful of cream and the chopped fresh mint.

CHILLED RASPBERRY AND CRANBERRY SOUP

This soup makes an unusual, refreshing first course. Rich ruby red, swirled with sour cream and sprinkled with fresh chopped mint, it looks really beautiful. It can be made very successfully with frozen raspberries, and the cranberry juice can be bought in large supermarkets and delicatessens. *Servies 4–6.*

1 package (10 ounces) frozen—
   or fresh—raspberries
3½ cups cranberry juice
2 tablespoons arrowroot

2–4 tablespoons sugar
Lemon juice
Sour cream—optional
2 tablespoons chopped fresh mint

Purée about two-thirds of the raspberries with some of the cranberry juice, then pass the purée through a sieve to remove the seeds. Put into a saucepan with most of the remaining cranberry juice and bring to the boil. Meanwhile, put the arrowroot into a small bowl and mix to a smooth cream with the rest of the juice. Pour the hot raspberry mixture over the arrowroot cream, stir, then return the mixture to the saucepan and stir over the heat until it has thickened. Remove from the heat and add the rest of the raspberries and a little lemon juice and sugar to taste. Cool, then chill the soup. When you're ready to serve the soup, ladle it into individual bowls. Stir the sour cream to make it smooth, then place a teaspoonful on each portion and sprinkle with the mint.

TOMATO AND FRESH BASIL SOUP WITH CREAM

When made from fresh tomatoes and basil from the garden, this has to be one of the best soups of all. If you don't have any basil, use chopped tarragon or chives instead. This is another soup I like chilled in the summer. *Serves 4–6.*

2 tablespoons butter or
  polyunsaturated margarine—or
  2 tablespoons oil if you're
  going to serve it chilled
1 onion, peeled and chopped
¾ pound potatoes, peeled and cut
  into even-size chunks
1 pound tomatoes, peeled and
  chopped

4½ cups light vegetable stock or
  water
Sea salt
Freshly ground black pepper
½ teaspoon sugar
⅔ cup light cream
2 tablespoons chopped fresh basil

Melt the butter in a large saucepan and add the onion; sauté for 5–7 minutes until fairly soft but not browned, then add the potatoes and cook for a further 2–3 minutes, stirring often. Put in the tomatoes, mix them round, then pour in the stock or water and bring up to the boil. Turn the heat down, put a lid on the saucepan and leave to simmer for about 20 minutes, until the potatoes are soft. Purée the soup and then pour it through a strainer into a clean saucepan to re-move the seeds of the tomatoes. Season with salt, pepper and sugar. Reheat and serve each bowlful topped with a swirl of cream and a sprinkling of basil.

Appetizers

FRUIT AND VEGETABLE FIRST COURSES

Artichokes with Sour-Cream Filling

Eggplant Fritters with Tomato Sauce

Avocado with Cottage Cheese and Cashew Balls
in Tomato Dressing

Surprise Avocados

Grapefruit Rose Baskets

Half Melons with Strawberries

Pineapple Wedges

•

PÂTÉS AND DIPS

Bean and Ripe-Olive Pâté with Hard-Boiled Eggs

Creamy Lima Bean Dip with Sesame Toast

Cheddar Cheese and Red Wine Dip

Quick Hummus

Sour-Cream and Herb Dip with Crudités

Stilton Pâté with Pears

Striped Pâté

Curried Vegetable and Nut Pâté with Yoghurt Sauce

FINGER FOOD: PASTRIES AND SANDWICHES

Hot Avocado Tarts

Baby Asparagus Tarts

Mushroom Patties with Yoghurt and Scallion Sauce

Miniature Open Sandwiches

Colored Pinwheels

Asparagus Rolls

Miniature Curried Lentil Balls with
Yoghurt and Sour-Cream Sauce

The first course sets the tone for the meal, whets people's appetite and gets things off to a good start. I particularly enjoy preparing this part of the meal because it's light and gives scope for imagination and fun.

However, on a more serious note, in a vegetarian meal this course does also provide an opportunity for introducing some extra protein if necessary, or a complementary protein, to make a nutritionally well-balanced meal. The Avocado with Cottage Cheese and Cashew Balls in Tomato Sauce, the Miniature Curried Lentil Balls, all the dips and pâtés, and the tarts contain substantial amounts of protein, and some of them can be served with salad to make light meals or snacks in their own right.

This chapter is divided into three sections: fruit and vegetable dishes; pâtés and dips; and pastries and sandwiches. The recipes in the last two sections are good to serve with drinks at parties, buffets and receptions (see pages 47–64).

Fruit and Vegetable
First Courses

ARTICHOKES WITH SOUR-CREAM FILLING

For this, the artichokes are cooked, cooled and served with a piquant, sour-cream and chive filling. They are messy to eat, so finger bowls or extra napkins are a good idea. *Serves 6.*

6 artichokes
⅔ cup sour cream
2 tablespoons mayonnaise
2 tablespoons chopped fresh
   chives

Sea salt
Freshly ground black pepper

First, to prepare the artichokes, wash them very well under cold running water, then cut the stems level with the base. Next take a pair of sharp scissors and snip the points off the leaves to square them off and make them less prickly to cope with. You will probably need two large saucepans for cooking the artichokes (or you could do them in two batches, as they're served cold). Put the artichokes into the saucepan and add enough cold water to cover them, bring to the boil and let them simmer, with a lid half on the pan, for about 40 minutes. They are done when you can pull a leaf off easily. Drain the artichokes and leave them upside down in a colander to drain and cool.

Meanwhile make the filling by simply mixing the sour cream and mayonnaise to a smooth consistency, then adding the chives and a little seasoning to taste.

When the artichokes are cold you will probably need to remove the inner prickly "choke." To do this, take the artichoke and pull back the leaves, like the petals of a flower, so that you can see the center. Take the soft central leaves in your hand and pull them away —they should come out quite easily—then use a teaspoon to scrape out any spiky center or choke. Rinse the artichoke to remove any remaining bits of choke, then dry the inside with a paper towel. Put the artichokes on individual plates, trimming the bases slightly if necessary to make them stand firm; then spoon the filling into the center, where the choke was, dividing it among them.

EGGPLANT FRITTERS WITH TOMATO SAUCE

This is one of the simplest ways of preparing eggplant, but one of my favorites, and I think it is tasty enough to serve as an extra course on its own: almost the equivalent of a fish course. The only disadvantage is that the eggplant does need to be fried just before serving, but this is quite a quick job and most of the preparation can be done well in advance. *Serves 6.*

1 large eggplant
Sea salt
Whole-wheat flour
Freshly ground black pepper
Olive oil for shallow frying
Grated Parmesan cheese

Lemon wedges
Watercress
2 cups homemade Tomato Sauce
   or Sour-Cream and Herb
   sauce or mayonnaise

Wash the eggplant and remove the stem, then cut the vegetable into ¼-inch slices. Put these into a colander, sprinkle them with salt and then place a plate and a weight on top and leave for at least 30 minutes. Afterward, rinse the pieces of eggplant under cold water and blot them gently with paper toweling to remove excess water. Dip the slices of eggplant in seasoned whole-wheat flour.

To finish the eggplant fritters, heat a little olive oil in a skillet and fry the slices, a few at a time, on both sides, until the outside is crisp and the inside feels tender when pierced with the point of a sharp knife. As the fritters are ready put them in a baking dish that has been lined with paper toweling and keep them warm in a cool oven until they are all ready. Serve the fritters sprinkled with a little grated Parmesan and garnished with wedges of lemon and sprigs of watercress. Serve the sauce separately.

AVOCADO WITH COTTAGE CHEESE AND CASHEW BALLS IN TOMATO DRESSING

This is an unusual appetizer: little balls of cottage cheese and roasted cashews served in a piquant tomato sauce with slices of avocado. The cheese balls and the dressing can be made in advance and stored in the fridge so that you only have to prepare the avocado and assemble the dish just before the meal. You can use roasted salted cashew nuts, but I prefer to buy plain ones and roast them by putting them on a dry baking sheet in a fairly hot oven for about 10 minutes, until they're golden brown. *Serves 6.*

FOR THE FILLING:

1 cup cottage cheese
¾ cup cashews, roasted and cooled
1 small garlic clove, crushed in a little salt

Sea salt
Freshly ground black pepper

FOR THE DRESSING:

½ teaspoon tomato paste
½–1 teaspoon sugar
¼ teaspoon paprika

2 tablespoons red wine vinegar
6 tablespoons olive oil

2 large ripe avocados
Juice of ½ lemon
2 tablespoons chopped fresh
  chives

*Crisp lettuce leaves and Melba
Toast*

Put the cottage cheese into a bowl and mash with a fork. Chop the cashews—a blender is good for this—and add to the cottage cheese, together with the crushed garlic and salt and pepper to taste. Mix well, then form into 24 small balls, about the size of hazelnuts. Leave on one side until ready to assemble the dish. (They can be made in advance and kept in a plastic container in the fridge.)

Make the dressing by mixing the tomato paste, sugar, paprika and vinegar; then gradually add the oil. Add some salt, pepper, and a little more sugar if necessary.

Just before you want to serve the meal, peel the avocados and remove the seeds. Cut the flesh into pieces and put them into a bowl with the lemon juice, chives and a little salt and pepper. Add the cheese and cashew balls. Mix everything very gently so that the ingredients are well distributed.

Arrange one or two crisp lettuce leaves on each serving dish and spoon the avocado mixture carefully on top. Give the tomato dressing another stir, then spoon a little over each plateful and serve immediately, accompanied by melba toast.

SURPRISE AVOCADOS

"Surprise," because the avocados are completely covered in a sharp, creamy, lemon mayonnaise dressing, and it isn't until you slice one that you find the buttery-soft avocado and the piquant herb filling in the center. You can make the filling and the dressing in advance, but don't prepare the avocados more than 1 hour ahead or they may discolor. *Serves 6.*

3 ripe avocados—*they should feel
just soft all over when you
cradle them in the palm of
your hand*
Juice of 1 lemon
½ cup cottage cheese
1 tablespoon finely chopped fresh
parsley
1 tablespoon finely chopped fresh
chives

Sea salt
Freshly ground black pepper
3 tablespoons mayonnaise
3 tablespoons plain yoghurt
Juice of ½ lemon
Lettuce leaves
Paprika
Lemon slices

Cut the avocados in half and remove seeds and skin. Brush the avocados all over with the lemon juice. To make the filling, mix the cottage cheese and the herbs, then season with a little salt and pepper. For the dressing, mix the mayonnaise and yoghurt.

To assemble the dish, put two or three small crisp lettuce leaves on each plate. Press a little of the cheese mixture into the cavity of each avocado half, dividing it among them. Put the avocados cut-side down on the lettuce leaves and pour the dressing over them. Sprinkle with paprika and garnish each plate with a wedge of lemon.

GRAPEFRUIT ROSE BASKETS

You may feel this is too romantic an idea, but I think you will agree it provides a conversation piece. I have to admit that I love it because it looks so pretty and different and is just the way to begin a celebration meal in summer. It consists of whole pink grapefruits, each skin cut into the shape of a basket (which is quite easy to do); then each basket is filled with the flesh that has been scooped out, chopped and mixed with rosewater and a few fresh pink rose petals, which are perfectly edible and taste delicious! For a final touch, each basket can be garnished with a small pink rosebud. You could make this in the spring using a few fragrant violets, which are also edible, and leaving out the rosewater.

6 pink grapefruits	Sugar
3–4 tablespoons rosewater	Rose leaves and, if possible, 6
A few pink rose petals	small pink rosebuds, for garnish

Using a sharp knife, make two cuts in the grapefruit about ⅛ inch each side of the stem, going halfway down the fruit. Insert the point of the knife at the base of one of these cuts and slice around, across the grapefruit until you get to the other cut. Remove the knife, then re-insert it the other side and repeat the process. These two sections of grapefruit should then fall away, leaving a basket shape. Now cut the fruit from the section under the "handle."

Remove the grapefruit flesh from the "bowl" of the basket in the usual way with a grapefruit knife. Prepare all the grapefruits in this manner, then cut the white skin and pith from the scooped-out chunks of fruit. Put this fruit into a bowl and add rosewater to taste, a few fresh rose petals, snipped with kitchen scissors or shredded, and just a very little sugar if you think it's needed.

Stand each grapefruit basket on a plate, cutting a slice from the base of the grapefruit if necessary to make it stand up, then spoon the rose petal mixture into the baskets. Tuck a few fresh rose leaves around the base of the baskets and lay a small pink rosebud on top of each basket, or alongside it on the plate.

HALF MELONS WITH STRAWBERRIES

Although it's so simple, I think this makes a perfect first course (or dessert) in summer. Any small, ripe, round melon will do. *Serves 6.*

3 small, ripe melons	Sugar—optional
2 cups strawberries, washed and	
hulled	

Cut the melons in half and scoop out the seeds. Put the melon halves on individual plates. Cut any large strawberries in halves or quarters so that they are roughly the same size. Put the strawberries in the center of the melons, dividing them among them. Serve with sugar, if desired.

PINEAPPLE WEDGES

A ripe, juicy pineapple makes a beautiful first course, especially before a rich meal. Look for a pineapple that's the right size to slice down in wedges, like a melon, and, if necessary, let it ripen for a day or two at room temperature. It's best if you prepare the pineapple just before you want to serve it. *Serves 6–8.*

1 large pineapple

Slice off the leafy top, cut the pineapple lengthwise in half, and then cut each half lengthwise again into three or four pieces. Put the wedges on individual plates, then slip a sharp knife between the flesh and the skin to loosen the flesh. Slice off any hard core, then cut the flesh down into segments that are the right size for easy eating.

Pâtés and Dips

BEAN AND RIPE-OLIVE PÂTÉ WITH HARD-BOILED EGGS

The olives give this dish a lovely salty piquancy and the bean and olive mixture is also very good just served with hot toast or thin whole-wheat bread and butter. *Serves 6.*

⅔ cup dried white beans: navy, cannellini or lima beans, soaked and cooked; or 1 can (16 ounces) lima beans
12 pitted ripe olives
2 tablespoons olive oil
2 tablespoons lemon juice
Sea salt

Freshly ground black pepper
Cayenne pepper
Crisp lettuce leaves
4 hard-boiled eggs
Paprika
Watercress
Lemon wedges

Drain the beans, reserving the liquid, and mash them to a purée—they needn't be too smooth. Mash the olives with a fork and add them to the beans, together with the oil and lemon juice. Stir in a little of the reserved liquid, if necessary, to make a soft creamy mixture the consistency of lightly whipped cream. Season with salt, pepper and a pinch of cayenne. Chill this mixture until required: it can be made several hours in advance.

Arrange two or three small crisp lettuce leaves in individual small bowls. Cut the eggs into wedges and put them on top, dividing them among the bowls. Spoon the bean and olive mixture on top and sprinkle with a little paprika. Decorate each bowl with a sprig or two of watercress and a wedge of lemon.

CREAMY LIMA BEAN DIP WITH SESAME TOAST

This is a creamy dip with a tangy flavor. It's an example of complementary proteins at work, because the wheat and sesame complement each other and the beans. If you use canned beans it's very quick to make and handy when friends drop by unexpectedly. *Serves 6.*

⅔ cup dried lima beans, soaked and cooked until tender, see page 23—or 1 can (16 ounces) lima beans
1 small garlic clove, peeled and crushed—optional
2 tablespoons olive oil
2–3 teaspoons lemon juice or wine vinegar

Sea salt
Freshly ground black pepper
Tabasco
Lettuce leaves
Lemon wedges
Watercress

FOR THE SESAME TOAST:

6 slices whole-wheat bread
Butter, softened

Sesame seeds

Drain the lima beans, reserving the liquid. Place them in a blender, adding enough of the reserved liquid to make a thick creamy purée; or mash them with a fork and beat in the liquid. Stir in the garlic, if you're using it, olive oil and enough lemon juice or wine vinegar to sharpen the mixture. Season well with salt and pepper and add a few drops of Tabasco. Chill the mixture, then just before you want to serve the dip, spoon it into individual ramekin dishes lined with lettuce leaves, and garnish with a wedge of lemon and a sprig of watercress. Serve with the hot sesame toast.

To make the sesame toast, set the oven to 400°F. Cut the crusts off the bread and roll each slice with a rolling pin to flatten it a bit. Spread the bread with butter and sprinkle a good layer of sesame seeds on top, pressing them in with the knife. Cut the bread into fingers and place on a baking sheet. Bake for 10–15 minutes, until crisp and golden brown. Serve at once with the creamy lima bean dip.

CHEDDAR CHEESE AND RED WINE DIP

The wine gives this dip an intriguing flavor and a pretty pink color. It's delicious for a special occasion, served with hot fingers of whole-wheat toast or slices of crisp melba toast. *Serves 6.*

2 cups finely grated Cheddar
  cheese
2 tablespoons soft butter or
  polyunsaturated margarine

½ cup dry red wine
½ teaspoon Tabasco
Freshly ground black pepper
Sea salt, to taste

Put the grated cheese into a bowl with the butter or margarine and the wine and beat them together to make a light, fluffy mixture. Add the Tabasco, pepper and a little salt if necessary—it may not need any as the cheese is quite salty. Spoon the mixture into a small bowl or dish and leave in a cool place until required. Serve with fingers of hot whole-wheat Sesame (see preceding recipe) or Melba Toast and butter.

QUICK HUMMUS

This is a quick version of hummus, made with canned chick peas. Normally I don't much like the sweet flavor and soggy texture of canned chick peas, but they are excellent for this dip. This is another very useful recipe for impromptu entertaining, either as a first course or for serving with drinks. *Serves 6.*

1 can (16 ounces) chick peas
1 garlic clove, peeled and crushed
1 tablespoon olive oil
2 teaspoons tahini (sesame seed
  paste)
2–3 teaspoons lemon juice

Sea salt
Freshly ground black pepper
Paprika
Extra olive oil
Lemon wedges

Drain the chick peas, reserving the liquid. Put the chick peas into a blender or food processor, adding enough of the reserved liquid to make a thick creamy purée; or mash them with a fork and beat in the liquid. Stir in the garlic, olive oil, tahini and enough lemon juice to sharpen the mixture, which should be fairly moist, like softly whipped cream. Season well with salt and pepper. Spread the mixture out on a plate so that it is only about ½ in. thick; smooth the top. Chill, if time permits. Just before you want to serve the hummus, sprinkle it with quite a generous amount of bright red paprika and drizzle a little olive oil over that. Put some lemon wedges around the edge. Let everyone help themselves to a spoonful and eat it with warmed pita-bread or soft, fresh whole-wheat bread or rolls.

SOUR CREAM AND HERB DIP WITH CRUDITÉS

Like the two preceding dips, this one can be made quickly. You can use any fresh green herbs or, if none are available, finely chopped scallions. *Serves 6.*

1 cup sour cream
1 small package (3 ounces) cream
  cheese
1 garlic clove, peeled and crushed
  —optional

2 tablespoons chopped fresh
  green herbs
Sea salt
Freshly ground black pepper

FOR THE CRUDITÉS:

A selection of three or more of the following:

Cauliflower florets
Small strips of red or green
  pepper
Scraped carrot sticks

Scallions or radishes, washed and
  trimmed—with the green part
  left on if it's presentable
Stalks of crisp celery

To make the dip, simply mix everything together and season with salt and pepper. Put the dip into a small bowl and serve with the crudités.

STILTON PÂTÉ WITH PEARS

The Stilton cheese gives this creamy log its lovely tangy flavor. I like to serve it on individual plates with slices of ripe pear and a few fresh walnuts, but it would also be very good served in a bowl with a selection of crudités. *Serves 6.*

1¼ cups finely grated Stilton
  cheese
1 cup cottage cheese
4 tablespoons milk

3 really ripe pears
Juice of 1 lemon
6 crisp lettuce leaves
¼ cup walnuts, chopped

Place the Stilton in a bowl with the cottage cheese and milk and mix well to a creamy consistency. Form the mixture into a fat sausage shape and wrap it in a piece of foil, twisting the ends. Chill the roll for at least 2 hours.

Just before you are ready to serve the log, peel and core the pears, then cut them into thin slices. Sprinkle the slices with the lemon juice, making sure they are all coated, to prevent their discoloring.

To serve, put a lettuce leaf on each plate and arrange the pear slices on top. Unwrap the log, cut the roll into six slices and put one on each plate on top of the pears. Sprinkle the walnuts on top and serve as soon as possible.

STRIPED PÂTÉ

This dish consists of different colored layers pressed into a loaf pan and chilled overnight. When turned out and sliced, it looks most attractive, yet it's very simple to make. Serve with crackers, or crisp melba toast. *Serves 6–8.*

FOR THE FIRST LAYER (YELLOW):

1½ cups grated Cheddar cheese
4 tablespoons butter or margarine,
   softened

4 tablespoons milk
Tabasco

FOR THE SECOND LAYER (GREEN):

½ cup ricotta cheese
1 medium-size ripe avocado

1 tablespoon lemon juice
Tabasco

FOR THE THIRD LAYER (WHITE):

1 cup ricotta cheese
1 large garlic clove, peeled and
   crushed—optional

TO FINISH:

6 stuffed green olives, halved
4 tablespoons finely chopped
   parsley or chives

Paprika
Watercress

First, fold some paper toweling into about eight layers to fit neatly into the base of an 8 x 4-inch loaf pan—this will absorb any liquid that seeps out of the pâté and ensure that it will be firm and easy to cut later. Then put a long strip of waxed paper on top of the paper towels, to cover the base and extend up the narrow sides of the pan.

Next, make the mixture for the first layer: put the grated cheese into a bowl and beat in the other ingredients to make a smooth cream. Season with salt, pepper and Tabasco.

For the avocado layer, put the cheese into a bowl and mash lightly with a fork. Cut the avocado in half and remove the seed and skin, then slice the flesh roughly and add to the ricotta cheese. Mash the avocado into the cheese, with the lemon juice, until you have a smooth green purée. Season with salt and pepper and add a few drops of Tabasco to taste.

To make the third layer, beat together the ricotta cheese and garlic, if you're using it, and add salt and pepper to taste.

To assemble the pâté, place the sliced olives, cut-side down, in the base of the pan, right down the center; then carefully spoon the yellow cheese mixture on top, pressing it down lightly and leveling it with the back of a spoon. Cover completely with the chopped parsley in a thick layer. Then spoon the avocado mixture on top and sprinkle with a thin but even layer of paprika. Cover this with the white layer of ricotta cheese, smooth with the back of a spoon, and then press another several thicknesses of paper toweling to cover. Put a weight on top and leave in the fridge overnight. (It's a good idea to replace the top layer of paper toweling with a new one after an hour or so, the first application will have absorbed a good deal of moisture.)

To serve the pâté, remove the toweling, slip a knife down the edges of the pan to loosen the contents, then invert the pan over a serving dish. Turn the pâté out and strip off the remaining layers of paper. The stuffed olives should now be on top, looking attractive against the yellow cheese mixture. Decorate with sprigs of watercress around the edge.

You need a sharp knife to cut the pâté into thick slices; this is a slightly tricky operation, so you may prefer to cut it first and serve it in slices on individual plates. Lay the slices flat to show off the pretty stripes, and decorate each with a sprig or two of watercress. It's also nice with the Yoghurt and Herb or Yoghurt and Scallion sauces on pages 152–53.

CURRIED VEGETABLE AND NUT PÂTÉ
WITH YOGHURT SAUCE

Another easy dish to make, this pâté consists of crunchy vegetables and nuts, flavored with curry and garlic. *Serves 6.*

2 tablespoons butter or
  polyunsaturated margarine
1 medium-size onion, peeled and
  finely chopped
1 carrot, scraped and finely
  chopped
1 stalk of celery, washed and
  chopped
½ green pepper, seeded and
  chopped

½ red pepper, seeded and chopped
1 garlic clove, peeled and crushed
1 tablespoon mild curry powder
1 cup chopped roasted hazelnuts,
  or filberts
1 cup cottage cheese
Sea salt
Freshly ground black pepper

FOR THE SAUCE:

¼ cup peeled and finely chopped
  cucumber
1 cup plain yoghurt
3 tablespoons finely chopped fresh
  mint

Salt
Pepper
Lettuce leaves
Sliced tomato

Line an 8 x 4-inch pan with a strip of waxed paper to cover the bottom and come up the two narrow sides. Melt the butter or margarine in a large saucepan and sauté the vegetables for 2–3 minutes: they should soften a little, but still be crunchy. Add the curry powder and cook for a further minute. Remove from the heat and stir in the rest of the ingredients. Spoon mixture into the prepared loaf pan—it won't fill it—and smooth the top. Cover with foil and chill for several hours.

Meanwhile make the sauce. Mix the cucumber with the yoghurt and mint. Season with salt and pepper.

When you're ready to serve the dish, put 2 or 3 small crisp lettuce leaves on individual plates. Slip a knife around the edges of the pâté to loosen it, then turn it out of the pan and cut into slices. Place one slice on each plate. Give the sauce a quick stir, then spoon a little over one corner of each portion of pâté; garnish the plates with sliced tomato. Serve the rest of the sauce in a small bowl or pitcher.

Finger Food:
Pastries and Sandwiches

HOT AVOCADO TARTS

To make these tarts, chunks of avocado are mixed with sour cream (or yoghurt for a less rich version) and heated through in crisp pastry shells. I think it's a delicious mixture of flavors and textures, but it's important not to let the avocados overheat or you will spoil the taste. However, the pastry shells can be made several hours in advance and just reheated and assembled, with the avocado, at the last minute. I use 4½-inch individual quiche/tart pans. This dish can also be made in an 8-inch quiche/tart pan and served either as an appetizer or a light main course. *Serves 6.*

FOR THE PASTRY:

1 cup whole-wheat flour
6 tablespoons polyunsaturated
  margarine or butter

¾ cup grated Swiss cheese
Sea salt
Freshly ground black pepper

FOR THE FILLING:

2 fairly large avocados
Juice of ½ small lemon
Sea salt
Freshly ground black pepper

⅔ cup sour cream, or plain
  yoghurt
2 tablespoons chopped fresh
  chives

First make the pastry: sift the flour into a large bowl, and just tip in the bran, which will be left in the sieve. Rub the margarine or butter into the flour using a pastry blender or a fork until the mixture resembles fine breadcrumbs. Add the grated cheese and some seasoning and press the mixture together to form a dough. If there's time refrigerate this dough for 30 minutes (this makes it easier to roll out but isn't essential).

Set the oven to 400°F, and if possible place a heavy baking sheet on the top shelf to heat up with the oven. Divide the pastry into six pieces and roll each out fairly thinly to fit the little tart pans; press the pastry into the pans, trim the edges and prick the bases. Put the tart shells into the oven on top of the baking sheet and bake for 15 minutes, until the pastry is lightly browned and set. Remove from oven and cool in pans on a wire rack. Lower oven temperature to 350°F.

To make the filling, cut the avocados in half and remove seeds and skin. Dice the flesh, sprinkle with the lemon juice and salt and pepper. Stir the sour cream into the avocado, turning the avocado so that it all gets coated with the cream, but don't mash it. Spoon the avocado mixture into the pastry shells, dividing it equally among them. Pop them into the oven for about 15–20 minutes to heat through, then sprinkle with chives and serve at once.

BABY ASPARAGUS TARTS

These are lovely for a party or as a first course. *Makes 12.*

FOR THE PASTRY:

2 cups whole-wheat flour
½ cup polyunsaturated
   margarine or butter

4–5 tablespoons cold water

12 *spears cooked fresh* or *frozen*
    asparagus or *canned asparagus,*
    drained and cut into 1-inch
    pieces
½ *cup grated Swiss cheese*

2 *eggs*
4 *tablespoons milk* or *light cream*
Sea salt
Freshly ground black pepper
Fresh parsley, chopped

To make the pastry, sift the flour into a large bowl and just tip in the bran that will be left in the sieve. Rub the margarine or butter into the flour, using a pastry blender or a fork, until the mixture resembles fine breadcrumbs. Add the cold water and press the mixture together to form a dough. If there's time, refrigerate this dough for 30 minutes (this makes it easier to roll out but isn't essential).

Preheat the oven to 400°F, and if possible place a heavy baking sheet on the top shelf to heat up with the oven. Roll out the pastry and ease it into the greased tartlet pans—it may be necessary to do these in two batches, depending on how many pans you have. Trim the edges and prick the bottoms. Put the shells into the oven on top of the baking sheet and bake for 15 minutes, until the pastry is lightly browned and set. Cool, then carefully remove the shells from the pans and place them on a baking sheet.

To finish the baby tarts, reduce the oven setting to 375°F. Put the pieces from one spear of asparagus in each little tart pan and sprinkle with some of the cheese. Whisk the eggs and milk or cream, add the remaining cheese and season to taste with salt and pepper. Spoon a little over each asparagus tart. Bake for about 15 minutes, until the filling is set. Sprinkle with chopped parsley before serving.

MUSHROOM PATTIES WITH YOGHURT AND SCALLION SAUCE

I make these in individual tart pans or shallow muffin pans. They are lovely as a first course, served warm with the chilled creamy sauce, or for a party, without the sauce. *Serves 6.*

FOR THE FILLING:

1 tablespoon butter or
  polyunsaturated margarine
1 tablespoon oil
1 medium-size onion, peeled and
  chopped
1 large garlic clove, peeled and
  crushed

1 pound mushrooms, sliced
1 tablespoon chopped fresh
  parsley
Sea salt
Freshly ground black pepper

FOR THE PASTRY:

2 cups whole-wheat flour
1 teaspoon dry mustard
¾ cup polyunsaturated
  margarine or butter

¾ cup grated Swiss cheese
Sea salt
Freshly ground black pepper

FOR THE SAUCE:

1 cup plain yoghurt
3 tablespoons light cream
3 tablespoons finely chopped
  scallions

Sea salt
Freshly ground black pepper

First prepare the filling. Heat the butter and oil in a large saucepan and sauté the onion for about 5 minutes, until it is beginning to soften; then add the garlic and mushrooms and sauté for a further 20–25 minutes until the mushrooms are very tender and all the liquid has boiled away, leaving them dry. Add the parsley and salt and pepper to taste. Remove from heat and leave them on one side to cool.

Meanwhile make the pastry: sift the flour and dry mustard into a large bowl, and just tip in the bran which will be left in the sieve. Add a little salt, then rub the fat into the flour using a pastry blender or a fork until the mixture resembles fine breadcrumbs. Mix in the grated cheese, then press the mixture together to form a dough, adding a very little cold water only if necessary. If there's time, leave this dough to rest in the fridge for 30 minutes (this makes it easier to roll out but isn't essential). Then roll out the pastry and use a round cutter to stamp out twenty-four circles to fit twelve shallow tart or muffin pans. Butter the pans well and line them with half of the pastry circles. Set the oven to 400°F.

Put a heaping teaspoonful of the mushroom filling into each pastry shell and place one of the remaining pastry circles on top, pressing down lightly; make a hole in the top of each to let the steam out. Bake the patties for about 15 minutes, until they are golden brown.

While the patties are cooking, make the sauce by mixing the yoghurt with the cream and scallions, and seasoning to taste with salt and pepper.

When the patties are done, carefully remove them from the pans and serve hot, with the sauce.

MINIATURE OPEN SANDWICHES

Open sandwiches look so pretty and I find they make an excellent appetizer with drinks or for a buffet. Make sure that the topping is pressed firmly onto the bread or else they can be rather messy to eat. Allow three to four for each person. These toppings are just ideas; you can of course vary them. *Makes 24–36 small open sandwiches.*

6 slices of dark rye bread or other
   flat firm bread

Butter
6–8 lettuce leaves

EGG AND OLIVE TOPPING:

2 hard-boiled eggs
2 tablespoons mayonnaise

8 pitted ripe olives
Watercress

TOMATO AND LIMA BEAN TOPPING:

1 (8 ounces) can lima beans
1 tablespoon olive oil
2 teaspoons lemon juice
Sea salt

Freshly ground black pepper
1 small tomato sliced thin
Fresh chives, chopped

AVOCADO TOPPING:

1 small avocado
Lemon juice
Sea salt
Freshly ground black pepper
2 tablespoons mayonnaise

1 small carrot, scraped and
   coarsely grated
Watercress
Paprika

Butter the slices of bread and cut each into four or six pieces. Press a piece of lettuce on top of each to cover and make a base for the toppings.

First make the egg and olive sandwiches: slice the hard-boiled eggs and arrange them on top of a third of the bread slices. Spoon a little mayonnaise over each and decorate with an olive and a little watercress.

For the tomato and lima bean sandwiches, drain the beans, reserving the liquid. Then make the beans into a paste by mashing them with the oil, lemon juice and about a tablespoonful of the reserved liquid to make a soft consistency. Season to taste with salt and pepper. Spoon this mixture on top of another third of the bread slices and decorate each with a tomato slice and some chopped chives.

Finally, for the avocado sandwiches, cut the avocado in half and remove the seed and skin. Put the avocado into a medium-size bowl with the lemon juice and mash until smooth. Season to taste with salt and pepper. Spoon this mixture onto the remaining pieces of lettuce-lined bread and top each with a little mayonnaise, a few shreds of grated carrot, a sprig of watercress and a dusting of paprika.

These look prettiest served on a large plate or wooden platter.

COLORED PINWHEELS

These pinwheels are good for serving at cocktail parties and similar functions: they look attractive, like slices from miniature savory swiss rolls. I like to make two batches, with contrasting fillings. *Makes about 50.*

10 *slices of firm whole-wheat*
    bread

FOR A GREEN FILLING:

½ *cup soft butter,*
    polyunsaturated margarine or
    ricotta cheese

4 *tablespoons finely chopped*
    fresh parsley
1 *tablespoon hot water*

1 cup finely grated Cheddar
  cheese
2 tablespoons butter or
  polyunsaturated margarine

2–3 tablespoons milk
Tabasco
Sea salt
Freshly ground black pepper

First make the fillings for the pinwheels. Beat together the butter, margarine, or ricotta cheese, parsley and hot water to make a light, creamy mixture. Put the Cheddar cheese into another bowl and beat in the butter or margarine and enough milk to make a soft consistency; add a drop or two of Tabasco and a little salt and pepper.

Cut the crusts off the bread and flatten each slice with a rolling pin. Spread half the slices generously with the green butter mixture and the rest of the slices with the orange mixture. Roll the slices up like swiss rolls and, if possible, chill them for an hour or so. Then cut each roll into about five fairly thin slices.

ASPARAGUS ROLLS

These are one of my favorite sandwich-type party foods: moist spears of asparagus rolled in thin whole-wheat bread. *Makes about 44.*

1 can (14½ ounces) asparagus
  tips, drained

1 loaf whole-wheat bread, sliced
Butter

Cut the crusts from the bread and roll each slice with a rolling pin to make it thinner and more flexible. Butter the bread. Put one spear of asparagus on each slice of bread and roll the bread around the asparagus. Cut each roll into two or three pieces so that they are a manageable size for eating. Keep in a cool place, covered with foil, until needed.

MINIATURE CURRIED LENTIL BALLS WITH YOGHURT AND SOUR-CREAM SAUCE

These little lentil balls can be served hot or cold; they make a delicious first course and are also good for a cocktail party or buffet. *Makes about 50, serves 6 as an appetizer.*

1 cup dried lentils
2½ cups water
2 tablespoons oil
1 onion, peeled and sliced
1 large garlic clove, peeled and
   crushed

2 teaspoons ground coriander
Sea salt
Freshly ground black pepper
Flour to coat
A little butter and oil for
   shallow-frying

FOR THE SAUCE:

2 tablespoons plain yoghurt
2 tablespoons mayonnaise
2 tablespoons sour cream

Sea salt, to taste
Freshly ground black pepper, to
   taste

TO SERVE:

Sprigs of watercress

Lemon slices

Put the lentils and water into a saucepan and bring to the boil, then turn down the heat and leave to cook very gently for 20 minutes, until soft. The lentils should be fairly dry so that they can be formed into balls; if they seem a bit on the wet side, leave the saucepan over the heat for a few minutes longer, stirring often.

Meanwhile heat the oil in a medium-size saucepan and sauté the onion for 10 minutes until softened and lightly browned. Add the garlic and coriander and cook for a further minute or two, then add the lentils and a good seasoning of salt and pepper. Let stand until cold, then form into small balls about the size of large hazelnuts and roll each in flour. Heat a knob of butter and a tablespoon of oil in a skillet and sauté the balls until they are crisp and brown. They are rather fragile and so need to be cooked carefully: I find it best to do only a few at a time. Drain the lentil balls on paper towels.

To make the sauce, simply mix everything together.

Serve the lentil balls hot or cold on small plates, garnished with lemon slices and watercress; or, for a buffet, put each little ball on a cocktail stick and serve on a plate or stuck into a grapefruit or cabbage. Offer the sauce in a small bowl so that people can help themselves to a spoonful and dip the lentil balls in it.

Salads

Apple Salad

Banana, Peanut and Scallion Salad

Beet, Apple and Celery Salad with Creamy Topping and Walnuts

Lima Bean, Tomato and Olive Salad

Carrot, Apple and Mint Salad

Cabbage Salad with Nuts and Raisins

Endive and Walnut Salad

Chinese Cabbage with Scallions

Fennel, Apple and Cucumber Salad

Green Herb Salad

Herb and Navy Bean Salad

Chunky Mixed Salad Bowl

Mushroom, Tomato and Avocado Salad Bowl

Potato Salad

Kidney Bean, Carrot and Walnut Salad

Molded Rice and Artichoke-Heart Salad

Tomatoes and Lima Beans in Basil Dressing

There are many cooked dishes for which I think the perfect accompaniment is simply a well-made salad, rather than cooked vegetables: the fresh flavor and crisp texture provide a pleasant contrast.

A salad is also much easier for the cook, especially when entertaining, because most of the work can be done beforehand. Although a green salad needs to be assembled and dressed at the last moment, the dressing can be made—I make mine straight into the wooden bowl from which I serve the salad—and the leaves left in a plastic bag in the fridge ready to be assembled in moments when you're ready. Then the salad can be tossed in the dressing at the table, by someone else, if you're busy.

Salads made from more robust ingredients, such as root vegetables, cabbage and cooked beans, can be made well in advance and are ideal for parties and other occasions when you want to get everything completely ready beforehand.

Most of the salads in this section are intended to be served with other dishes, rather than as main salad meals, though the two bean salads and the rice salad are rich in protein and make attractive, simple meals on their own or as part of a selection of cold dishes for a party.

APPLE SALAD

This salad consists of a colorful, crunchy mixture of apples, carrots, celery, nuts and raisins, with a creamy dressing on top. It's good served with warm whole-wheat rolls and cheese for a simple meal. *Serves 4–6.*

3 red apples, cored and finely diced
3 large carrots, scraped and finely diced
1 bunch of celery, washed and finely diced
½–1 cup walnuts, coarsely chopped
½–1 cup raisins
2 tablespoons chopped fresh chives
Juice of 1 orange
Lettuce leaves
1 cup sour cream

Put the apple, carrot, celery, nuts, raisins and chives into a large bowl and add the orange juice. Stir the mixture to make sure that everything is coated with the juice. Line a large dish or shallow salad bowl with lettuce and spoon the apple mixture on top. Spoon the sour cream over the top of the salad, so that some of the pretty mixture still shows underneath. Serve as soon as possible.

BANANA, PEANUT AND SCALLION SALAD

This salad goes very well with Asian or Indian dishes because it contains some of the foods most often served with them—banana, salted peanuts, coconut. But putting everything together in one big bowl is much easier than preparing numerous courses and makes an interesting and unusual salad. *Serves 4.*

2 *large bananas*
Juice of 1 orange
1 *bunch scallions, trimmed and*
   chopped
1 *medium-size red pepper,*
   seeded and chopped

2 *tablespoons plain yoghurt or*
   mayonnaise or a mixture
1 *cup salted dry or roasted*
   peanuts (see page 22)
1 *tablespoon shredded coconut*

Peel and slice the bananas, then put them into a bowl and add the orange juice. Add the scallion, red pepper and yoghurt or mayonnaise and mix everything together. Just before serving, add the peanuts so that they stay crunchy, and sprinkle with the coconut.

BEET, APPLE AND CELERY SALAD WITH CREAMY TOPPING AND WALNUTS

This pleasant mixture of flavors and textures goes well with a cold nut pâté or nut roast. *Serves 4–6.*

¾ *pound cooked beets*
2 *crisp, sweet, eating apples*
1 *heart of celery*

1 *cup ricotta cheese*
2 *tablespoons milk*
½ *cup chopped walnuts*

Rub the skins off the beets, then rinse. Cut the beets into chunks. Peel, core and dice the apples; slice the celery. Mix the beets with the apple and celery and put on a serving dish or into a salad bowl.

Next, to make the creamy topping, put the ricotta cheese into a bowl and beat in the milk to make a smooth, creamy consistency. Pour this over the beet mixture and sprinkle with the chopped walnuts.

LIMA BEAN, TOMATO AND OLIVE SALAD

This succulent mixture makes a very good protein-rich salad, but it also makes a lovely light lunch or supper when served with warm whole-wheat rolls or French bread to sop up the juices. *Serves 4.*

3 tablespoons olive oil
1 tablespoon wine vinegar
Sea salt
Freshly ground black pepper
1 medium-size onion, peeled and
    sliced
1 pound tomatoes, skinned and
    sliced

1 can (16 ounces) lima beans,
    drained; or ⅔ cup dried lima
    beans, soaked, cooked and
    drained
8–10 pitted ripe olives

Put the oil and vinegar in a wooden salad bowl and add a little salt and freshly ground black pepper. Then add the onions, tomatoes, lima beans and olives, and toss everything gently to mix the ingredients, making sure that all the flavors blend.

CARROT, APPLE AND MINT SALAD

The fresh mint gives this salad a curiously sweet, aromatic flavor I find delicious. It is especially good with cheese dishes. *Serves 4.*

3 tablespoons olive oil
1 tablespoon wine vinegar
Sea salt
Freshly ground black pepper
¾ pound carrots
½ pound Savoy cabbage

3 sweet, eating apples
2 heaping tablespoons chopped
    fresh chives
2 heaping tablespoons chopped
    fresh mint

First make the dressing very simply by putting the oil and vinegar in a wooden salad bowl and mixing it with a little salt and freshly ground black pepper.

Next, scrape the carrots and dice finely; wash and shred the cabbage; dice the apples, discarding the cores. Put the carrots, cabbage and apples into the bowl, together with the chopped chives and mint and mix well.

CABBAGE SALAD WITH NUTS AND RAISINS

This crunchy, colorful salad is perfect for those occasions when you want a salad that can be prepared ahead and won't wilt and spoil. This one actually improves with time! *Serves 4.*

3 tablespoons olive oil
1 tablespoon wine vinegar
Sea salt
Freshly ground black pepper
2 cups shredded Savoy cabbage
1 cup scraped and coarsely
   grated carrots
1 medium-size red pepper,
   seeded and chopped

2 heaping tablespoons chopped
   fresh chives, parsley or
   scallions
½ cup raisins
½ cup roasted peanuts (see page
   22)

First make the dressing very simply by putting the oil and vinegar in a wooden salad bowl and mixing it with a little salt and freshly ground black pepper. Add all the ingredients except the peanuts and mix well, so that everything gets coated with the shiny dressing. Stir in the peanuts just before serving, so that they stay crisp.

ENDIVE AND WALNUT SALAD

Walnut oil gives this salad a delicious nutty flavor and blends very well with the slight bitterness of the endive.

Serves 4–6.

1 pound endive
3 tablespoons olive oil, or, if you
  can get it, half walnut oil and
  half olive oil

1 tablespoon wine vinegar
Sea salt
Freshly ground black pepper
½ cup coarsely chopped walnuts

Wash the endive, dry carefully, then slice. Put the oil and vinegar into a salad bowl, add some salt and pepper and mix together. Add the endive and walnuts and toss them in the dressing until everything is well coated. Serve at once.

CHINESE CABBAGE WITH SCALLIONS

This salad is made in the same way as the endive one above, using Chinese cabbage leaves and adding a bunch of chopped scallions instead of (or, if you prefer, as well as) the walnuts. I also rather like it with raisins too; they add a pleasant touch of sweetness.

FENNEL, APPLE AND CUCUMBER SALAD

I especially like this salad with pasta and with cheese dishes. Small portions served on a bed of lettuce also make a good first course, with thinly sliced whole-wheat bread and butter. *Serves 4.*

1 bulb of fennel—about 12
  ounces
3 apples, peeled, cored and diced
½ cucumber, peeled and diced

2 tablespoons mayonnaise
4 tablespoons plain yoghurt
Sea salt

Wash and trim the fennel, removing the tough outer leaves and pieces of stem, but keeping any feathery leaves for the garnish. Slice the fennel quite finely. Put the fennel into a bowl and add the apples, cucumber, mayonnaise, yoghurt and a little salt to taste, and gently mix everything together. Chop the reserved feathery leaves and sprinkle over the top.

GREEN HERB SALAD

A green salad can be adapted to whatever herbs are in season, and is perhaps the most useful basic salad of all. I think plenty of fresh herbs make all the difference, and I personally like to make my salad quite pungent with garlic and onion rings, but leave these out if they're not to your taste. *Serves 4.*

3 tablespoons olive oil
1 tablespoon wine vinegar
Sea salt
Freshly ground black pepper
1 garlic clove, peeled and
  crushed—optional
1 medium-size head of lettuce,
  washed, shaken dry and
  shredded

Other greens, as available:
  watercress; sliced endive,
  fennel or cucumber; finely
  shredded tender spinach
2 heaping tablespoons chopped
  fresh herbs, as available:
  parsley, chives or scallions,
  mint, tarragon, basil
1 onion, peeled and sliced into
  rings—optional

First make the dressing very simply by putting the oil and vinegar in a wooden salad bowl and mixing it with a little salt, freshly ground black pepper and the garlic if you're using it. Add all the other ingredients and toss well, so that everything is coated with the shiny dressing. Serve immediately.

HERB AND NAVY BEAN SALAD

This salad is best made at least a couple of hours before you need it so that the beans have time to absorb the flavors of the herbs. This salad is best served chilled, for lunch or supper, with just some warm bread and chilled white wine. *Serves 4–6.*

6 tablespoons olive oil
2 tablespoons wine vinegar
1 teaspoon sugar
½ teaspoon dry mustard
1–2 garlic cloves, peeled and
   crushed
Sea salt

Freshly ground black pepper
1⅓ cups dried navy beans, soaked,
   cooked and drained
2 heaping tablespoons chopped
   fresh herbs, as available:
   parsley, chives or scallions,
   mint, tarragon, basil

First make the dressing very simply by mixing the oil, vinegar, sugar, mustard and garlic, if you're using it, in a wooden salad bowl and adding a little salt and freshly ground black pepper. Add all the other ingredients and toss well, so that everything is coated with the shiny dressing. You can add the beans while they are still warm and the salad will be all the better for it, because the beans will absorb the dressing and flavorings better.

CHUNKY MIXED SALAD BOWL

It's best if you can find a really hearty lettuce for this salad: a romaine, for example, so that you can break it into nice chunky pieces.

The other ingredients are largely a matter of personal taste and can be varied according to what is available or in season. *Serves 4.*

3 tablespoons olive oil
1 tablespoon wine vinegar
1 garlic clove, peeled and
   crushed—optional
Sea salt
Freshly ground black pepper
1 large head of lettuce, washed
   and torn into chunky pieces

4 firm tomatoes, cut into wedges
½ cucumber, cut into chunks
1 small bunch of celery or endive
   sliced
1 tablespoon fresh chives or
   scallions, chopped
1 onion, peeled and sliced into
   rings—optional

First make the dressing very simple by putting the oil and vinegar into the base of a wooden salad bowl and mix with a little salt, freshly ground black pepper and the garlic if you're using it. Add all the other ingredients and mix well, so that everything gets coated with the shiny dressing. Serve immediately.

MUSHROOM, TOMATO AND AVOCADO SALAD BOWL

If you can get those small, very fresh, white mushrooms, they make a lovely salad that I especially like served with pasta tossed in a little olive oil and sprinkled with grated Parmesan. *Serves 4.*

2 ripe avocados
Juice of ½ lemon
3 tablespoons olive oil
1 tablespoon wine vinegar
Sea salt
Freshly ground black pepper

½ pound tomatoes, skinned and
   sliced
½ pound fresh mushrooms,
   washed and sliced
1 tablespoon chopped fresh
   chives or scallions

First cut the avocados in half and remove seeds and skin. Dice the flesh into ½-inch pieces and sprinkle with the lemon juice. Put the oil and vinegar in a wooden salad bowl and add a little salt and freshly ground black pepper. Then add the tomatoes, mushrooms, avocado and chives and toss everything gently to mix the ingredients and make sure that all the flavors blend. Serve as soon as possible.

POTATO SALAD

If it's well made, with firm chunks of potato in a creamy dressing, potato salad is delicious and is a good choice for a buffet. *Serves 6, or more if served with other salads.*

1½ pounds new potatoes
Sea salt
2 rounded tablespoons
  mayonnaise

2 rounded tablespoons plain
  yoghurt
Freshly ground black pepper
Fresh chives or parsley, chopped

Cook the potatoes in boiling salted water until they are just tender: for the best flavor, cook them in their skins and then slip off the skins with a sharp knife. Cut the potatoes into chunks and put them into a bowl. Mix together the mayonnaise and yoghurt, and add some salt and pepper to taste. Add this to the potatoes, turning them gently with a spoon until they are all coated in the creamy dressing. Serve cold, with some fresh chives or parsley snipped over the top.

KIDNEY BEAN, CARROT AND WALNUT SALAD

The grated carrots in this salad provide interesting color contrast while the walnuts add texture as well as providing extra protein. This salad is nourishing enough to be a light meal, along with slices of whole-wheat bread and butter and some fruit. *Serves 4.*

⅔ cup dried red kidney beans or	Sea salt
1 can (16 ounces) drained	Freshly ground black pepper
3 tablespoons olive oil	1 tablespoon chopped scallions
1 tablespoon wine vinegar	1 cup coarsely grated carrots
1 teaspoon sugar	½ cup chopped walnuts
½ teaspoon dry mustard	
1 small garlic clove, peeled and	
crushed—optional	

If you're using dried red kidney beans, cover them with cold water and leave them to soak for at least 2 hours; then drain and rinse them. Put the beans into a saucepan and cover with fresh water; bring up to the boil and allow the beans to boil vigorously for at least 10 minutes. Then lower the heat and leave them to simmer, with a lid on the saucepan, until tender—about 1 hour. Drain.

Meanwhile make the dressing by putting the oil, vinegar, sugar, mustard and garlic, if you're using it, in a wooden salad bowl and mixing them with a little salt and freshly ground black pepper. Add all the other ingredients, except the nuts, and mix well, so that everything is coated with the shiny dressing. You can add the beans while they are still warm and the salad will be all the better for it because they will absorb the dressing and flavorings particularly well. Stir in the nuts just before serving so that they stay crunchy.

MOLDED RICE AND ARTICHOKE-HEART SALAD

This is a pretty salad of rice with pale green artichoke hearts, mushrooms and red pepper, made in a ring-shape with the center filled with a glossy, golden egg mayonnaise sprinkled with toasted almonds. You could serve the salad more simply, if you prefer, just spooned onto a plate, but for a special occasion it does look attractive in the ring shape, and it's not difficult to do. *Serves 6–8, or more if served as part of a selection of salads.*

1¼ cups brown rice
2½ cups water
Sea salt
4–6 tablespoons oil
1 large onion, peeled and chopped
½ pound fresh mushrooms,
   washed and sliced
2 large garlic cloves, peeled and
   crushed

2 medium-size red peppers,
   seeded and cut into long slices
   about ¼ inch wide
8 whole mushrooms, stalks
   removed
1 can (14½ ounces) artichoke
   hearts, drained and quartered
Freshly ground black pepper

FOR THE FILLING:

6 hard-boiled eggs
3 tablespoons mayonnaise
3 tablespoons plain yoghurt

¾ cup slivered almonds, toasted
Watercress

Put the rice in a medium-size, heavy saucepan and add the water and a level teaspoon of sea salt. Bring to the boil, give the rice a quick stir, then cover the saucepan, turn the heat down and leave the rice to cook very gently for 45 minutes. Take the sucepan off the heat and let stand, still covered, for a further 15 minutes.

While this is happening, heat 2 tablespoons of the oil in a large saucepan and sauté the onion for 5 minutes, until softened; then add the mushrooms and garlic and cook for a further 20–25 minutes, stirring from time to time, until all the liquid has evaporated.

Heat the rest of the oil in another small saucepan or frying pan and sauté the red pepper, for about 5 minutes, just to soften it a little. Remove the red pepper from the oil and quickly sauté the eight mushroom caps, adding a little extra oil if necessary. Drain on paper towels.

Oil a large 2-quart ring mold and arrange the mushroom caps and strips of red pepper alternately in the bottom. The mushrooms should be put in black side down, and the red pepper strips should be placed so that they extend a bit up the sides. You won't need all the red pepper, so chop up what you don't use, also any mushrooms that are left over.

Mix the sliced mushrooms, remaining red pepper and artichoke hearts with the cooked rice and season well. Spoon this rice mixture into the ring mold, pressing it down well. Cover the ring with a piece of foil and chill until needed.

For the filling, chop the eggs into chunky pieces and mix them gently with the mayonnaise and yoghurt. To serve the dish, turn the rice mold out onto a large round serving dish. Quickly stir most of the almonds into the egg mayonnaise mixture and spoon this into the center, heaping it up well. Sprinkle the rest of the almonds over the egg mixture and tuck a few sprigs of watercress round the sides of the ring.

An excellent variation is to use 1 pound small leeks, cut into 1-inch pieces, cooked and drained, instead of the artichoke hearts.

TOMATOES AND LIMA BEANS IN BASIL DRESSING

In this salad the beautiful pale green of the beans looks very pretty with the red tomato and chopped green basil. If you can't get fresh basil, use chopped chives or the green tops of scallions. *Serves 4–6.*

1 package (16 ounces) frozen
   lima beans
1 pound tomatoes
2 tablespoons olive oil
1 tablespoon wine vinegar

1 tablespoon chopped fresh basil
Sea salt
Freshly ground black pepper
Lettuce leaves

Cook the beans in a little fast-boiling water until just tender, then drain and cool.

Peel and slice the tomatoes, removing any hard pieces from the core. Put the oil, vinegar and basil into a bowl and mix together, then add the tomatoes, beans and some salt and pepper. Mix gently, so that everything is evenly coated with the oil and vinegar. If possible let stand for 2 hours for the beans to absorb the flavors fully. To serve, line a shallow bowl with a few lettuce leaves and spoon the bean mixture on top.

Accompanying Vegetables

Spiced Beets with Apples and Cranberries

Brussels Sprouts with Chestnut and Wine Sauce

Festive Brussels Sprouts

Purée of Brussels Sprouts

Buttered Cabbage with Garlic and Coriander

Chinese Cabbage with Scallions

Red Cabbage with Apples Baked in Cider

Oven-Baked Carrots

Braised Cucumber with Walnuts

Fennel with Egg Sauce

Buttered Snow Peas with Sugar and Mint

Gratin Dauphinois

Potato and Almond Croquettes

Potatoes in Herbs

Baked Potatoes with Sour Cream

Potatoes with Lemon

Garlic Potatoes

Potato Purée

Potato and Turnip Purée

Potato and Celeriac Purée

Ratatouille

Root Vegetables in Turmeric and Coconut Sauce

Spiced Rice

Onion Rice

The vegetable dishes in this section are mainly fairly simple ones for serving as accompaniments to main dishes, though some of them, such as the braised cucumber with walnuts and the fennel in creamy egg sauce, make good first courses on their own, and the ratatouille is also handy as a filling for crêpes and as a base for the Brown Nut Rissoles in Tomato Sauce on page 127.

Some of these vegetable dishes, especially the purées, ratatouille and the baked red cabbage, are particularly useful for serving with savory nut loaves and pies, as they are moist enough to take the place of both a vegetable and a sauce, making them not only simple and delicious but also time saving.

I have also included two ways of preparing savory rice, which is good served with vegetable casseroles and spiced bean dishes.

SPICED BEETS WITH APPLES AND CRANBERRIES

This is an excellent mixture of flavors and very easy to make. It's moist and good for serving with a savory loaf such as the Lentil, Hazelnut and Cider Loaf (page 122). *Serves 6.*

1 pound sweet apples	1 pound cooked beets
½ cup cranberries	Sea salt
2 tablespoons sugar	Freshly ground black pepper
¼–½ teaspoon ground cloves	

Peel, core and slice the apples. Wash and pick over the cranberries, removing any stems. Put the apples and cranberries into a small, heavy saucepan with the sugar and cook over a gentle heat, with a lid on the saucepan, for about 10 minutes, until soft and mushy. Mash the fruits with a spoon, or purée them if you prefer a smooth sauce. Add the ground cloves, then taste and add more sugar if necessary.

Meanwhile rub the skins off the beets with your hands; wash the beets under cold water then cut into chunky pieces. Add these to the sauce, together with some salt and pepper. Leave over a very gentle heat for 10–15 minutes to give the beets time to heat through and absorb the flavors.

BRUSSELS SPROUTS WITH CHESTNUT AND WINE SAUCE

There's nothing new about the mixture of Brussels sprouts and chestnuts, but this is a different way of combining the two flavors: nutty small sprouts served with a smooth chestnut sauce. It's lovely at Christmas or for a special winter meal. *Serves 4–6.*

1 tablespoon butter	1 cup stock or half stock and half
1 tablespoon oil	red wine
1 large onion, peeled and chopped	Sea salt
1 small garlic clove, peeled and	Freshly ground black pepper
crushed	1½ pounds Brussels sprouts—
½ cup canned chestnut purée	small ones if possible

First make the sauce. Heat the butter and oil in a medium-size saucepan and sauté the onion for 10 minutes until soft but not browned.

Add the garlic, chestnut purée, stock or stock and wine, and some salt and pepper and cook for a further few minutes, to give the flavors a chance to blend; then purée and adjust the seasoning with a little more stock or wine if necessary. Put the sauce back into the saucepan and keep it warm over a very low heat.

Wash and trim the Brussels sprouts. Leave them whole if they're tiny; otherwise halve or quarter them. Put ½ inch water into a saucepan and bring to the boil; add the sprouts, bring up to the boil again and cook for 5–7 minutes—until they are just tender. Drain at once.

Put the Brussels sprouts into a warmed serving dish and pour a little of the sauce over them, but don't cover them completely. Serve the rest of the sauce separately.

FESTIVE BRUSSELS SPROUTS

This is a recipe for cheering up sprouts toward the end of the season when they are cheaper in price but you're tired of them! It's a very colorful mixture that goes well with many main courses. *Serves 4–6.*

1½ pounds Brussels sprouts—
    small ones if possible
½ pound carrots
2 tablespoons oil
1 large onion, peeled and chopped
1 garlic clove, peeled and
    crushed

1 small red pepper, seeded and
    sliced
1 tablespoon chopped parsley
Sea salt
Freshly ground black pepper

Wash and trim the Brussels sprouts. Leave them whole if they're tiny; otherwise halve or quarter them. Scrape the carrots and dice them. Put ½ inch water into a saucepan and bring to the boil. Add the sprouts and carrots, bring up to the boil again and cook for 5–7 minutes—until the vegetables are just tender. Drain at once.

Meanwhile heat the oil in a medium-size saucepan and sauté the onion, garlic and red pepper for about 7 minutes, or until tender. Add this vegetable mixture to the sprouts and carrots, together with the salt and pepper to taste.

PURÉE OF BRUSSELS SPROUTS

This is an excellent way to serve the larger Brussels sprouts; it's light and delicate in flavor. For a less rich version you can use a little of the cooking liquid or some milk instead of some or all of the cream. *Serves 4–6.*

1½ pounds Brussels sprouts
1 tablespoon butter
⅔ cup light cream

Sea salt
Freshly ground black pepper
Grated nutmeg

Wash and trim the Brussels sprouts, then cook them in a little fast-boiling salted water for about 10 minutes, until they are tender. Drain the sprouts thoroughly and then purée them in a blender or food processor. Pour the purée back into the saucepan and add the butter. Beat in enough cream to make a soft purée. Season with the salt, freshly ground black pepper and grated nutmeg. Reheat gently.

BUTTERED CABBAGE WITH
GARLIC AND CORIANDER

This is a simple way of enhancing ordinary cabbage. The garlic and coriander make it taste good enough for a special occasion. *Serves 4.*

1½–2 pounds firm cabbage,
   washed and shredded
Sea salt
Freshly ground black pepper
Grated nutmeg
1–2 large garlic cloves, peeled and
   crushed

2 teaspoons coriander seeds,
   crushed
1 tablespoon butter or
   polyunsaturated margarine

Put about ½ inch water into a large saucepan, bring up to the boil, then add the cabbage. Let the cabbage simmer gently, covered, for 7–10 minutes, until it is just tender. Drain the cabbage well in a colander, then put it back into the saucepan and add salt, freshly ground pepper and grated nutmeg to taste. Mix the crushed garlic, coriander and butter or margarine together, and then add this to the cabbage, mixing it thoroughly. Serve at once.

CHINESE CABBAGE WITH SCALLIONS

If you prepare the cabbage and scallions in advance and keep them in a plastic bag in the fridge, this dish can be made very quickly, in about 5 minutes, just before the meal. *Serves 4–6.*

1 Chinese cabbage, about 1½–2
   pounds
1 large bunch scallions
2 tablespoons oil
1 tablespoon chopped fresh
   parsley

Sea salt
Freshly ground black pepper
Sugar

Wash the cabbage and shred it—not too finely. Wash, trim and chop the scallions, keeping as much of the green part as seems reasonable. All this can be done in advance.

Just before the meal, heat the oil in a fairly large saucepan and add the cabbage and scallions. Turn them in the oil, over a fairly high heat for about 3 minutes, until the cabbage has softened just a little but is still crisp. Add the chopped parsley and some salt, pepper and perhaps a dash of sugar to taste. Serve at once.

RED CABBAGE WITH APPLES
BAKED IN CIDER

This red cabbage dish will cook gently in the oven without any attention and is so moist and juicy that you don't need to serve a sauce with the meal. The fruity cider goes particularly well with the apples and cabbage, but it would also be good made with red wine, or you could leave out the alcohol altogether and use stock or water. *Serves 4–6.*

1½ pounds red cabbage	3 tablespoons oil
2 large onions, peeled and chopped	1¼ cups apple cider
	1½ teaspoons sea salt
2 large cooking apples, peeled, cored and chopped	Freshly ground black pepper
	1 teaspoon sugar

Shred the cabbage with a sharp knife, cutting out and discarding any hard central core. Put the cabbage into a large saucepan, cover with cold water and bring to the boil; then drain the cabbage in a colander.

Meanwhile sauté the onions and apples in the oil in a large saucepan for 5–10 minutes. Add the cabbage, cider and salt, pepper and sugar to taste. Bring up to the boil, then either turn the heat down low and leave the cabbage to cook very gently, covered, for about 1½ hours; or transfer the mixture to an ovenproof casserole, cover and bake in a warm oven, 325°F, for about 2 hours. Stir the mixture from time to time to help it cook evenly.

This dish reheats well—and I also like it cold.

OVEN-BAKED CARROTS

I find it very convenient to be able to cook a vegetable dish in the oven, to avoid last-minute preparations, especially when I'm entertaining. This is a lovely way to prepare carrots and seems to retain all their flavor. If you want to bake these carrots at the same time as something else, they can be baked on the lower rack of a hotter oven if necessary. *Serves 6.*

1 ½ *pounds carrots—baby ones are especially nice*
½ *pound pearl onions*
2 *tablespoons butter* or *polyunsaturated margarine*

Juice of 1 lemon
½ *teaspoon sugar*
Sea salt
Freshly ground black pepper
Fresh parsley, chopped

Set the oven to 325°F. Scrape the carrots and, if you're using baby ones, leave them whole; otherwise cut the carrots into even-size pieces. Peel the onions and halve or quarter any large ones. Use half the butter or margarine to grease an ovenproof dish generously. Put the carrots and onions in the dish and add the lemon juice, sugar and a little salt and pepper. Dot the remaining butter over the surface. Cover and bake for about 45 minutes, until the vegetables are tender. Taste and add more sugar, salt and pepper if necessary. Then sprinkle with the chopped parsley and serve from the dish.

BRAISED CUCUMBER WITH WALNUTS

People are sometimes surprised at the idea of cooking cucumber, but it's delicious, tender and palest green, with a delicate flavor. *Serves 6.*

2 *large cucumbers*
Sea salt
2 *tablespoons butter* or *polyunsaturated margarine*
1 ¼ *cups water*

1 *tablespoon lemon juice*
1 *bay leaf*
6 *peppercorns*
¼ *cup coarsely chopped walnuts*

Peel the cucumbers, cut them into 2-inch chunks, then cut each chunk down into quarters. Put the chunks into a colander, sprinkle with salt and leave under a weight for about 30 minutes to draw out the excess liquid. Rinse and drain. Melt the butter in a fairly large saucepan, then add the cucumber chunks, water and lemon juice, bay leaf and peppercorns. Bring up to the boil, then leave to simmer for 10–15 minutes, until the cucumber is tender and looks translucent and most of the liquid has evaporated, leaving the cucumber glistening in just a little buttery stock. If there is more than 2 or 3 tablespoons of liquid, turn up the heat and let it bubble away. Put the cucumber and the liquid into a warmed, shallow casserole or serving dish and sprinkle with the chopped walnuts.

FENNEL WITH EGG SAUCE

I think this creamy egg and nutmeg sauce goes perfectly with the slightly licorice flavor of fennel. This makes an excellent accompanying vegetable, but it is also a very good course on its own, perhaps served in little individual ovenproof dishes. *Serves 4–6.*

3 large bulbs of fennel—about	*1 hard-boiled egg, finely chopped*
1½ pounds	*2 tablespoons sour cream*
1¼ cups water	*Freshly ground black pepper*
Sea salt	*Grated nutmeg*

Trim the fennel and slice the bulbs into quarters or eighths. Put the water and a little salt into a saucepan; bring to the boil then add the fennel and simmer for 20–30 minutes, until the fennel feels tender when pierced with the point of a sharp knife. Remove the fennel with a draining spoon, put it into a shallow, heatproof casserole dish and keep it warm. Let the water in which the fennel was cooked boil rapidly until it has reduced to just a couple of tablespoonfuls. Then take the saucepan off the heat and stir in the chopped hard-boiled egg and the sour cream. Add salt, pepper and grated nutmeg to taste. Spoon this sauce over the fennel and serve immediately. Large, sweet onions are also very good cooked this way.

BUTTERED SNOW PEAS
WITH SUGAR AND MINT

For a simple vegetable dish, I think this is hard to beat. Snow peas have such a lovely, delicate flavor and are easy to cook. Like ordinary shelled peas, they are, I think enhanced with a little sugar and some chopped fresh mint. *Serves 6.*

1½ pounds snow peas	*Sea salt*
1 tablespoon butter	*Freshly ground black pepper*
½–1 teaspoon sugar	*1 tablespoon chopped fresh mint*

Put about 1 inch of water into a fairly large saucepan and bring to the boil. Add the peas and let them cook gently for 3–5 minutes, until they are just tender. Drain them, then return them to the hot saucepan and add the butter, sugar, salt and pepper to taste and the chopped mint. Mix gently, so that all the peas are coated with the butter and seasonings.

GRATIN DAUPHINOIS

Here is my less rich version of this delicious traditional dish: I have found that by using a creamy, low-fat, white cheese, such as ricotta, instead of some of the cream, you can have a luxurious-tasting result that's light and low in calories. I find this potato dish goes well with many things and is extremely easy to make. *Serves 4–6.*

2 tablespoons butter or	*1 garlic clove, peeled and*
polyunsaturated margarine	*crushed*
1½ pounds potatoes	*Sea salt*
½ cup ricotta cheese	*Freshly ground black pepper*
⅔ cup light cream	*Grated nutmeg*

First prepare a shallow, ovenproof dish by greasing it generously with half the butter or margarine. Preheat the oven to 325°F.

Next, peel the potatoes, then slice them very finely. Put the potato slices into a colander and wash them thoroughly under cold water to remove some of the starch; pat them dry on paper towels. Mix together the ricotta and cream. Stir in the garlic and a good seasoning of salt, pepper and grated nutmeg. Arrange a layer of the potato slices in the prepared dish and season with salt, pepper and some grated nutmeg. Spoon a layer of the cheese mixture on top, then cover with another layer of potatoes; continue in this way until all the potato and cheese mixture are used, ending with a layer of the latter. Dot the rest of the butter over the top, then cover with a piece of foil and bake for 1½–2 hours, until the potatoes feel tender when pierced with the point of a knife. Remove the foil and serve straight from the dish.

This can be baked on the lower rack of a hotter oven if you want to cook other things at the same time.

POTATO AND ALMOND CROQUETTES

This mixture of creamy potatoes and crunchy almonds is delicious, and these crisp little croquettes make a good accompaniment to many dishes. They are useful for entertaining because they can be made in advance and then baked in the oven. They also make a light meal, served with a herby green salad or tomato salad, in which case this quantity will be right for four. *Serves 6 as an accompaniment, 4 as a light meal.*

1½ pounds potatoes	¼ cup slivered almonds
2 tablespoons butter or	Sea salt
polyunsaturated margarine	Freshly ground black pepper
4 tablespoons milk	Extra ground almonds for coating
¼ cup ground almonds	Oil

Peel and boil the potatoes; when they're nearly done, preheat the oven to 400°F. Mash the potatoes with the butter or margarine and enough milk to make a light but firm mixture. Add the ground and slivered almonds and season well with salt and pepper. Form into about twelve little sausages. Roll the potato croquettes in the extra ground almonds so that they are completely coated. Put the croquettes on an oiled baking sheet and bake for about 30 minutes, turning them after 15 minutes, until they are crisp and golden brown. Serve immediately.

POTATOES IN HERBS

New potatoes are best for this recipe. You need to use a really generous amount of herbs so that their flavor fully permeates the potatoes and makes them delicious. *Serves 4–6.*

3 tablespoons butter or
    polyunsaturated margarine
A good bunch of fresh herbs:
    whatever is available, including
    some thyme

1½ pounds new potatoes,
    scrubbed
Sea salt
Freshly ground black pepper

Preheat the oven to 325°F. Grease an ovenproof casserole with half the butter or margarine, then lay half the herbs on the bottom. Add the potatoes and cover with the remaining herbs and butter. Season with salt and pepper. Cover the casserole and place it in the oven for about 45 minutes, or until the potatoes are tender when pierced with a sharp knife. Serve from the casserole, but remove the herb sprigs and leaves first.

BAKED POTATOES WITH SOUR CREAM

These baked potatoes are delicious with a vegetable casserole, such as Red Cabbage and Apples Baked in Cider (page 88), and they are also a good addition to a vegetarian barbecue. *Serves 4.*

4 medium-size potatoes
A little oil
Sea salt

Freshly ground black pepper
⅔ cup sour cream

Preheat the oven to 450°F. Scrub the potatoes and cut away any blemishes, as necessary. Make a long cut down the center of each to allow the steam to escape and provide an opening for the sour cream later. Rub each potato in a little oil, put them in a baking pan and place in the oven. Bake the potatoes for 1–1¼ hours, until they feel tender when squeezed gently.

When the potatoes are done, open up the slit in the top by pulling the potatoes apart slightly with your hands and sprinkle a little salt and pepper inside the potato. Stir the sour cream with a spoon to make it smooth, then put a heaping teaspoonful on top of each potato. Serve at once.

POTATOES WITH LEMON

Many dishes are enhanced by the taste of lemon, and one way of providing this is to flavor the accompanying potatoes with lemon. In this recipe, the potatoes are boiled until almost tender, then mixed with melted butter, lemon juice and grated rind and heated through in a fairly hot oven until they're sizzling and golden. *Serves 6.*

1½ pounds potatoes
2 tablespoons butter or
   polyunsaturated margarine,
   softened

Grated rind of 1 small lemon
1 tablespoon lemon juice
Sea salt
Freshly ground black pepper

Preheat the oven to 350°F. Peel the potatoes; cut them into fairly small even-size chunks and cook in boiling water for about 15 minutes, until they are just tender—don't let them get too soft. Spread the potatoes out in a shallow ovenproof casserole dish, then dot them with the butter or margarine and sprinkle with the lemon rind and juice and some salt and pepper. Bake the potatoes for about 40 minutes, turning them several times, until they are golden. Serve at once, from the dish.

GARLIC POTATOES

This variation of Potatoes with Lemon (see previous recipe) is also delicious. Prepare the potates as described for Potatoes with Lemon, but leave out the lemon. Crush one or two large garlic cloves and mix this paste into the butter before dotting it over the potatoes. Turn the potatoes thoroughly two or three times during the cooking to make sure that the garlic is well distributed.

POTATO PURÉE

A purée of potatoes (or other vegetables) can take the place of a sauce with dishes that need something moist to go with them. You can make this mixture rich and creamy to serve with a fairly plain main dish or just mash the potatoes with some of their cooking water and add plenty of butter and freshly ground black pepper. *Serves 6.*

1½ pounds potatoes
2 tablespoons butter
⅔ cup light cream or milk—
  optional

Sea salt
Freshly ground black pepper

Peel the potatoes, cut them into even-size pieces and boil them until tender. Drain thoroughly, reserving the water. Mash the potatoes by hand or in a food processor and then return them to the saucepan, over a low heat. Add the butter and gradually beat in enough cream, milk or reserved cooking water to make a light, fluffy mixture, softer than mashed potatoes. Season with plenty of salt and freshly ground black pepper.

POTATO AND TURNIP PURÉE

Follow the instructions for Potato Purée (page 95), using half potatoes and half turnips, or two-thirds turnips to one-third potatoes.

POTATO AND CELERIAC PURÉE

This is a very pleasant variation of the basic Potato Purée. I think it's best made with two parts celeriac to one part potatoes.

RATATOUILLE

Ratatouille is a useful dish because it can be made in advance and reheated; it is also excellent as a filling for crêpes or with lasagne. The exact composition can of course be varied according to what is available; cucumber makes a pleasant replacement for some of the eggplant or zucchini. *Serves 6.*

1 pound zucchini, diced
1 pound eggplant, diced
Sea salt
3 tablespoons olive or other
 vegetable oil
2 large onions, peeled and
 chopped

2–4 large garlic cloves, peeled
 and crushed
2 red peppers, seeded and sliced
4 large tomatoes, peeled and
 sliced
Freshly ground black pepper
Chopped parsley

Put the diced zucchini and eggplant into a colander and sprinkle with salt; then place a plate and a weight on top and leave for at least half an hour for any bitter liquids and excess moisture to be drawn out. Rinse under cold running water and blot as much liquid with paper towels as you can.

Heat the oil in a large saucepan, add the onions and sauté them for 7–10 minutes, until they're beginning to soften; then add the garlic, peppers and zucchini/eggplant mixture. Stir the vegetables so that they are coated with oil, then put a lid on the saucepan, turn down the heat and leave them to cook gently for 30 minutes. Next, stir in the tomatoes, put the lid back on, and leave over a gentle heat for a further 20–30 minutes. Season with salt and plenty of freshly ground black pepper. Sprinkle with chopped parsley before serving.

ROOT VEGETABLES IN TURMERIC AND COCONUT SAUCE

This is a beautiful dish of orange and gold root vegetables, bathed in a creamy, delicately flavored sauce. *Serves 6.*

1 cup shredded coconut
1½ cups milk
½ pound carrots
½ pound turnips
½ pound parsnips
2 tablespoons oil
1 onion, peeled and chopped

1 garlic clove, peeled and crushed
1 teaspoon grated fresh
 gingerroot
1 teaspoon turmeric
½ green pepper, seeded and sliced
Sea salt
Freshly ground black pepper

Heat the milk to boiling, then pour it over the coconut, leaving it to infuse while you prepare the vegetables. Scrape the carrots, peel the turnips and parsnips and cut them into even-size chunks. Heat the oil in a medium-size saucepan and sauté the onion for 7–10 minutes; then stir in the garlic, ginger and turmeric and cook for a further 2 minutes. Add the root vegetables, turning them with a spoon so that they all are coated with the spicy onion mixture. Strain the milk mixture over them, pressing the coconut against the sieve to extract as much flavor as possible (the coconut can now be discarded). Add the green pepper and some salt and pepper to taste, then put the saucepan over a low heat, cover and leave the vegetables to cook very gently for about 15–20 minutes, until they feel tender when pierced with the point of a knife.

SPICED RICE

Although rice is not really a vegetable, I'm including this recipe here because so many people substitute rice for potatoes, and it goes well with many of the other dishes in this book. *Serves 4–6.*

2 tablespoons oil	3 cloves
1 onion, peeled and chopped	3 cardamom pods
1 large garlic clove, peeled and	1 bay leaf
crushed	2½ cups boiling water
1¼ cups long grain brown rice	Sea salt
1 teaspoon turmeric	Freshly ground black pepper

Heat the oil in a heavy saucepan and sauté the onion for 7–10 minutes, until tender but not browned. Then add the garlic, rice and spices and sauté for 1–2 minutes, stirring all the time. Next pour in the boiling water and add a seasoning of salt and pepper. When the mixture is boiling vigorously, give it a stir, then turn the heat right down and put a lid on the saucepan. Leave to cook very gently for about 45 minutes, then remove from the heat and let stand, still covered, for a further 10 minutes. Fluff the rice gently, removing the bay leaf and spices before serving.

ONION RICE

For this variation of the above, simply leave out all the spices and season carefully with salt and pepper.

Main Courses

BAKED, STUFFED AND EN CASSEROLE

Asparagus in Hot Lemon Mayonnaise

Hot Avocado with Wine Stuffing

Lima Bean and Cider Casserole

Lentil and Mushroom Burgers

Spiced Lentils

Stuffed Zucchini Baked with Butter and Thyme

Mushroom Rice with Almonds and Red Pepper

Stuffed Red Peppers with Almonds

Tomatoes Stuffed with Pine Nuts

Salsify with White Wine and Mushrooms

Spinach Roulade

Spiced Vegetables with Dhal Sauce

Baked Crêpes with Leeks

Cheese Fondue

NUT LOAVES AND RISSOLES

Chestnut, Sage and Red Wine Loaf

Lentil, Hazelnut and Cider Loaf

Pine-Nut Loaf with Herb Stuffing

White Nut Loaf with Capers

White Nut Rissoles Baked with Mushrooms

Brown Nut Rissoles in Tomato Sauce

Nut Rissoles in Ratatouille

Vegetarian Scotch Eggs

PIES, QUICHES, PIZZAS AND PASTA

Asparagus Quiche

Eggplant, Red Pepper and Cheese Quiche

Cauliflower, Stilton and Walnut Quiche

Deep-Dish Mushroom Pie

Deep-Dish Vegetable Pie

Flaky Mushroom Roll

Mushroom Pudding

Walnut Pâté en Croûte

Special Pizza

Individual Pizzas

Lentil Lasagne

Spaghetti with Lentil and Wine Sauce

The main vegetable dishes in this section range from elegant and summery stuffed avocados and asparagus with lemon mayonnaise, to hearty bean casserole and spiced vegetables, which are warming and filling for the winter.

All these vegetable dishes are quite easy to make; the Spinach Roulade sounds complicated but isn't, and some of the recipes, particularly the stuffed tomatoes, avocados and red peppers, also cook quickly and are useful for those occasions when you have to produce a meal on the spur of the moment.

The choice of vegetables to have with a main vegetable dish requires care to ensure that the meal contains enough contrast and interest. Sometimes I think it's best to serve the main course on its own or with a simple potato dish followed by a crisp salad.

Baked, Stuffed and En Casserole

ASPARAGUS IN HOT LEMON MAYONNAISE

This is a delicious main course for the early summer when you want to make the most of the asparagus season. The hot asparagus is coated with a lemon mayonnaise mixture, sprinkled with bread crumbs and heated through just enough to warm the sauce and make the crumbs crisp. I think it's best served on its own or just with buttered new potatoes, followed by a refreshing green salad before cheese or a fruit tart. *Serves 4.*

2¼ *pounds fresh or frozen*
  asparagus
6 *rounded tablespoons homemade*
  or good-quality bought
  mayonnaise
1 *cup sour cream*
Lemon juice

Dijon-style mustard
Sea salt
Freshly ground black pepper
1 *cup soft whole-wheat bread*
  crumbs
½ *cup grated cheese (Parmesan*
  or Swiss are best)

If you're using fresh asparagus, trim off the hard stems—these ends are too tough to eat but can be used to make a stock for asparagus soup. Wash the asparagus gently to remove any grit. The easiest way to cook asparagus (if, like me, you haven't got a proper asparagus steamer) is in an ordinary steamer; otherwise you can stand the asparagus up in a bunch in a saucepan containing ½ inch water and arrange a piece of foil over the top to make a domed cover—this way the tougher ends of the stalks cook in the water and the delicate tops are steamed. Either way, the asparagus will take about 10 minutes to cook: it should be *just* tender. Frozen asparagus is best cooked in a steamer and takes 7–10 minutes.

While the asparagus is cooking, make the sauce by mixing together the mayonnaise and sour cream. Sharpen with a little lemon juice and mustard and season with salt and freshly ground black pepper. If the mixture seems a bit on the thick side, stir in a tablespoon or two of the asparagus cooking water.

Preheat the oven to 300°F. Put the asparagus into a large, shallow ovenproof dish and pour the sauce over the top. Cover completely with a thin layer of fine whole-wheat crumbs and sprinkle with the cheese. Bake in the oven for about 30–40 minutes until heated through: the crumbs can be browned quickly under the broiler afterward, if necessary. The dish should not be overcooked or the sauce may curdle.

HOT AVOCADO WITH WINE STUFFING

This avocado dish makes a delicious, luxurious main course. Make sure that the avocados are really ripe—they should just yield to fingertip pressure all over. It's important to leave the preparation of the avocados until the last minute, and only just warm them through in the oven, though the filling can be made in advance. *Serves 6.*

1 cup finely grated brazil nuts
1 cup grated Swiss cheese
1 cup soft whole-wheat bread
   crumbs
1 can (8 ounces) tomatoes

1 small garlic clove, peeled and
   crushed
1 tablespoon tomato paste
2 tablespoon chopped fresh
   chives

4–6 tablespoons dry sherry	3 ripe avocados
Sea salt	Juice of 1 lemon
Freshly ground black pepper	A little extra grated cheese and
Tabasco	bread crumbs for topping

First make the stuffing: put the nuts, cheese, bread crumbs, tomatoes, garlic, tomato paste and chives into a bowl and mix together. Stir in enough sherry to make a soft mixture that will just hold its shape, then season with salt and plenty of pepper and enough Tabasco to give the mixture a pleasant tang. Leave to one side until just before the meal—you can make the stuffing a few hours ahead if convenient.

Preheat the oven to 450°F. Just before the meal, halve the avocados and remove the skin and seeds. Mix the lemon juice with a good pinch of salt and a grinding of pepper and brush all over the avocados. Place the avocados in a shallow ovenproof dish. Spoon the stuffing mixture into the avocados, dividing it evenly among them; sprinkle a little cheese and a few bread crumbs on top of each. Put the avocados into the oven and turn the heat down to 400°F. Bake the avocados for 15 minutes. Serve immediately. (I find it best to put the avocados into the oven just as everyone sits down for their first course—it's important that they not be overcooked.) They are delicious with Potato Purée (page 95) and a lightly cooked vegetable, such as baby carrots.

LIMA BEAN AND CIDER CASSEROLE

This is lovely served with hot crusty rolls or potatoes baked in their skins and sprinkled with grated cheese. If you have a large, flameproof casserole dish, it is ideal for making this; otherwise you will have to sauté the vegetables in a saucepan first and then transfer them to an ovenproof dish to finish cooking.

A variation is to put medium-large peeled potatoes, one for each person, into the pot with the lima beans and vegetables and cook them together. Cooked this way, the potatoes soak up the flavors and are delicious, but you need a large casserole dish. *Serves 4.*

1 tablespoon butter or margarine
1 tablespoon oil
3 large onions, peeled and sliced
2 garlic cloves, peeled and crushed
1 pound carrots, scraped and sliced
1¼ cups dried lima beans, soaked, cooked and drained; or 2 cans (16 ounces each) lima beans, drained

1¼ cups stock or vegetable broth
⅔ cup apple cider or dry white wine
Bouquet garni
Sea salt
Freshly ground black pepper

Preheat the oven to 325°F. Heat the butter or margarine and oil in a large ovenproof saucepan and add the onions and garlic. Sauté for 5 minutes, browning them slightly, then stir in the carrots and cook for a further 4–5 minutes, stirring frequently to prevent sticking. Add the lima beans, stock, cider, bouquet garni and a little salt and pepper. Bring up to the boil, then cover and transfer to the oven to cook for 1½–2 hours. If you want a slightly thicker gravy, stir in a teaspoon of cornstarch or arrowroot blended with a little stock and let the mixture boil for a minute or two to thicken. Remove bouquet garni before serving.

LENTIL AND MUSHROOM BURGERS

The mushrooms make these burgers moist while the lentils add texture and protein. The burgers hold together well and can be cooked in the oven on a greased baking sheet, fried on top of the stove or grilled over a barbecue. I like them with a dollop of creamy Béarnaise sauce—or mayonnaise—and fresh watercress; but they are also lovely when eaten in a soft roll with lots of mustard or chutney. *Serves 4.*

1 tablespoon butter
1 tablespoon oil
1 onion, peeled and chopped
1 pound mushrooms, washed and
  chopped
2 large garlic cloves, peeled and
  crushed
¾ cup lentils, cooked and very
  well drained

2 tablespoons fresh parsley,
  chopped
Sea salt
Freshly ground black pepper
Flour for coating
Oil

If you're going to bake the burgers in the oven, preheat it to 400°F. Heat the butter and oil in a large saucepan and sauté the onion for 5 minutes, until it begins to soften; then add the mushrooms and garlic. Sauté over a moderate heat for 20–25 minutes, until all the liquid has evaporated and the mushrooms are reduced to a thick purée. Stir them from time to time while they are cooking. Take the saucepan off the heat and mix in all the other ingredients, seasoning to taste with salt and pepper. Form the mixture into burger shapes and roll the burgers lightly in flour. Place them on a greased baking sheet and bake for about 30 minutes, turning them over halfway through the cooking time. (Alternatively, fry the burgers quickly in a little hot oil, or brush them with oil and grill on both sides.)

SPICED LENTILS

This is a simple casserole of lentils baked with butter, garlic and coriander. It goes well with the Spiced Rice on page 98, the Root Vegetables in Turmeric and Coconut Sauce on page 97, and a salad. Serves 4–6.

3 tablespoons oil
2 large onions, peeled and sliced
4 large garlic cloves, peeled and
  crushed
4 teaspoons ground coriander

1¼ cups lentils, soaked and
  drained, (see page 23)
1¼ cups water
Sea salt
Freshly ground black pepper

Preheat the oven to 325°F. Heat the oil in a large, flameproof casserole dish and add the onion; sauté for 5 minutes, until the onion is beginning to brown and soften, then mix in the garlic and coriander and cook for a further 2–3 minutes, stirring. Add the lentils and stir them so that they all are coated with the oil and spice, then pour in the water. Bring up to the boil, cover and place in the oven for 40–60 minutes, until the lentils are tender and have absorbed the water. Season with salt and pepper.

STUFFED ZUCCHINI BAKED WITH BUTTER AND THYME

Zucchini can be hollowed out, stuffed and baked in butter and herbs, rather as you might bake a chicken. The result is delicious and one of my favorite summer and autumn dishes. Try serving it with Apple and Cranberry Sauce, roast potatoes and spinach. *Serves 4–6.*

1 large zucchini, about 2¼
   pounds, or several smaller ones
1 cup soft bread crumbs
1 cup butter
Juice and grated rind of 1 small
   lemon
1 teaspoon marjoram

½ cup chopped fresh parsley
1 egg
Sea salt
Freshly ground black pepper
2 tablespoons butter
3–4 teaspoons thyme

Preheat the oven to 350°F. Peel the zucchini, keeping it whole. Cut a slice off one end and reserve. Scoop out the seeds to leave a cavity for stuffing. Make the stuffing by mixing together the bread crumbs, butter, lemon juice and rind, marjoram, parsley and egg; season with salt and pepper. Push this mixture into the cavity of the zucchini, then replace the reserved end and secure with a skewer. Rub the butter all over the outside of the zucchini and sprinkle with 2–3 teaspoons of the crushed thyme. Put the vegetable in an ovenproof dish, sprinkle with

1 teaspoon thyme, cover loosely with a piece of aluminum foil and bake for about an hour, or until the zucchini is tender and can be pierced easily with the point of a knife. Serve with fresh Tomato Sauce or Special Wine Sauce.

MUSHROOM RICE WITH ALMONDS AND RED PEPPER

The secret of this recipe is to use plenty of mushrooms and to cook them thoroughly, separately from the rice, so that you get a really rich flavor and a tender, moist texture. This is a nice easy-going dish because, if necessary, you can cover it with foil and keep it warm for a while in a cool oven. It only really needs some grated Parmesan and a well-dressed green salad to go with it, though I must admit that for a special occasion I also like it with a rich Béarnaise sauce! There is some protein in the almonds, rice and Parmesan, but for a well-balanced meal it would be a good idea to introduce more protein, either in the first course or the dessert, or add little cubes of cheese or cooked beans to the salad. *Serves 4–6.*

1¼ cups long-grain brown rice
2½ cups vegetable stock
1 teaspoon sea salt
2 tablespoons butter
3 tablespoons oil
1 large onion, peeled and chopped
2 pounds fresh mushrooms, washed and sliced
2 large garlic cloves, peeled and crushed

½ cup slivered almonds
1 medium-size red pepper, seeded and chopped
Sea salt
Freshly ground black pepper
Fresh parsley, chopped
Parmesan cheese, grated

Put the rice into a medium-size, heavy saucepan and add the stock and sea salt. Bring to the boil, give the rice a quick stir, then cover the saucepan, turn the heat right down and leave the rice to cook very gently for 45 minutes. Then take the saucepan off the heat and let it stand, still covered, for a further 15 minutes.

While this is happening, heat the butter and 1 tablespoonful of the oil in a large saucepan and sauté the onion for 5 minutes, until softened; then put in the mushrooms and garlic and cook for a further 20–25 minutes, stirring from time to time, until all the liquid has evaporated and the mushrooms are dark and glossy.

Heat the rest of the oil in another small saucepan or skillet and first sauté the almonds until golden, then take them out and place on a paper towel. Quickly sauté the red pepper, for about 5 minutes, just to soften it a little.

To complete the dish, add the mushrooms, red peppers and almonds to the cooked rice, using a fork to avoid mashing the rice. Season carefully with salt and plenty of freshly ground black pepper. Spoon the mixture onto a large warmed plate or shallow ovenproof dish and sprinkle with freshly chopped parsley. Serve with Parmesan cheese.

STUFFED RED PEPPERS WITH ALMONDS

Red peppers are delicious stuffed with a tasty filling of mushrooms, wine, bread crumbs, nuts and tomatoes. Serve them with Potato Purée (page 95) and a green vegetable. *Serves 6.*

3 medium-large red peppers
1 cup chopped almonds
1 cup grated Cheddar cheese
1 cup soft whole-wheat bread crumbs
1 can (8 ounces) tomatoes
¼ pound mushrooms, washed and chopped
½ cup stock, red wine or dry cider

1 garlic clove, peeled and crushed
Sea salt
Freshly ground black pepper
A little extra grated Cheddar cheese and bread crumbs for topping

Preheat the oven to 375°F. To prepare the peppers, halve them and remove the center and seeds; rinse them under cold water. Put them into a saucepan half filled with cold water and bring them up to the boil. Remove from the heat, drain and place in a lightly greased, shallow ovenproof dish.

Next make the stuffing: put the nuts, cheese, bread crumbs, tomatoes, mushrooms, stock (or wine or cider) and garlic into a bowl and mix together, adding salt and pepper to taste. Spoon this mixture into the peppers, dividing it among them. Sprinkle with crumbs and grated cheese. Bake, uncovered, for about 40 minutes, until the peppers are tender and the stuffing golden brown.

TOMATOES STUFFED WITH PINE NUTS

I cannot make this dish without thinking of summer holidays in France because it's something I've made so often at the end of a hot sunny day there, with big tomatoes and fragrant thyme from the market. These tomatoes are delicious with Onion Rice (page 99) or buttered noodles and a green salad. You should be able to get pine nuts easily: if not, or if you think they're too extravagant, use chopped cashews instead. *Serves 4.*

4 *large tomatoes, about 2 pounds*	1 *garlic clove, peeled and crushed*
Sea salt	2 *tablespoons chopped fresh*
2 *tablespoons olive oil*	*parsley*
1 *onion, peeled and finely chopped*	1 *tablespoon fresh thyme or 1 teaspoon dried*
¾–1 *cup pine nuts*	*Freshly ground black pepper*
2 *cups soft whole-wheat bread crumbs*	

Preheat the oven to 375°F. Wash the tomatoes, slice off the tops (reserving them) and scoop out the seeds with a spoon—they will not be needed for this recipe, although they can be made into a good sauce to serve with it, following the recipe for fresh Tomato Sauce, page 153.

Sprinkle the inside of the tomatoes with a little salt and place them upside down in a colander to drain while you prepare the stuffing. To do this, heat the oil in a saucepan and sauté the onion for about 7 minutes, until softened, then remove from the heat and stir in the pine nuts, bread crumbs, garlic, parsley and thyme; season. Arrange the tomatoes in a lightly greased, shallow ovenproof dish and fill each with some of the nut mixture, dividing it among the tomatoes. Then replace the sliced-off tops, if you like, and bake, uncovered, for 20–30 minutes, until they're tender.

SALSIFY WITH WHITE WINE AND MUSHROOMS

Salsify has a delicate flavor said to slightly resemble that of oysters. I don't know how much truth there is in this, having never tasted oysters, but I do like the flavor of salsify, which I think is very pleasant and delicate. Cooked like this, with a wine-flavored lemon mayonnaise sauce, a topping of crisp crumbs and a garnish of fresh lemon, it's excellent either as a first or main course. If you're serving this as a main course, I think it goes best with just a simply cooked green vegetable such as zucchini, spinach or snow peas; or just buttered new potatoes, followed by a refreshing green salad before the cheese or dessert course. *Serves 4.*

2¼ pounds salsify
3 tablespoons lemon juice
Sea salt
Freshly ground black pepper
6 tablespoons mayonnaise,
   homemade or good-quality
   bought
1 cup sour cream

4 tablespoons dry white wine
Dijon-style mustard
½ pound small mushrooms,
   wiped and trimmed
1 cup soft whole-wheat bread
   crumbs
½ cup grated Swiss cheese

Peel the salsify and cut into 1-inch pieces. As they're prepared, put them into a saucepan containing 4 cups cold water and 2 tablespoons of the lemon juice—this will help to keep them white. When they're all prepared, put the saucepan on the heat, bring to the boil and cook for about 10 minutes, or until the salsify feel tender when pierced with the point of a knife. Drain, sprinkle with the remaining lemon juice and season with salt and pepper.

While the salsify is cooking, make the sauce by mixing the mayonnaise, sour cream, white wine and a dash of mustard if desired. Season with salt and freshly ground black pepper.

Preheat the oven to 400°F. Put the salsify into a large shallow ovenproof dish and add the mushrooms; pour the sauce over the top. Cover completely with the crumbs and cheese and bake for 30–40 minutes, until heated through. (Timing will depend partly on the depth of the dish you've used, but the mixture shouldn't be overcooked or the sauce may separate.) If the top isn't crisp enough, finish it off quickly under the broiler. Serve at once.

SPINACH ROULADE

This is good served with buttered new potatoes or Potatoes with Lemon, Tomato Sauce and baby carrots. *Serves 4–6.*

2 *pounds fresh spinach or 2 packages (10 ounces each) chopped frozen spinach*	*Freshly ground black pepper*
1 *tablespoon butter*	*Grated nutmeg*
Sea salt	4 *eggs, separated*
	A little grated Parmesan cheese

FOR THE FILLING:

¼–½ *pound mushrooms*	1 *teaspoon corn starch or arrowroot*
1 *tablespoon butter*	1 *cup light cream*

First prepare the spinach. If you're using fresh spinach, wash it thoroughly and put it into a large saucepan without any water. Put a lid on the saucepan and cook the spinach for 10 minutes, until it's tender, and then drain and chop. Cook frozen spinach according to the directions on the package, and drain well. Add the butter and seasoning and stir in the egg yolks.

Line a shallow 7 x 11-inch baking dish with greased waxed paper to cover the bottom and sides. Sprinkle with the Parmesan cheese. Preheat the oven to 400°F. Whisk the egg whites until stiff but not dry and fold them into the spinach mixture. Pour the mixture into the prepared dish and bake for 10–15 minutes, until risen and springy to the touch.

While the roulade is cooking, make the filling. Wipe and slice the mushrooms and sauté them in the butter for 5 minutes, until tender. Mix together the corn starch or arrowroot and cream; add this to the mushrooms and stir over the heat briefly, until slightly thickened. Season with salt, pepper and nutmeg. Keep the mixture warm but don't let it boil.

Have ready a large piece of waxed paper dusted with Parmesan cheese and turn the roulade out onto this; strip off the bottom paper used during baking. Spread the filling over the roulade, then roll it up jelly-roll fashion and slide it onto a warmed serving dish. Return to the oven for 5 minutes to heat through, then serve immediately.

SPICED VEGETABLES WITH DHAL SAUCE

This is a lovely dish, not hot but lightly spiced. The dhal sauce supplies the protein and it's nice served with Spiced Rice (page 98), pappadums, mango chutney and the Banana, Peanut and Scallion Salad on page 68. *Serves 4.*

3 tablespoons oil
1 onion, peeled and chopped
1 large clove garlic, peeled and crushed
1 teaspoon turmeric
1 teaspoon ground coriander
1 teaspoon ground cumin
1 bay leaf

2 carrots, about ½ pound, scraped and thinly sliced
1 pound potatoes, peeled and cubed
2 leeks, washed and sliced
⅔ cup water
Sea salt
Freshly ground black pepper

FOR THE DHAL SAUCE:

1 onion, peeled and chopped
1 clove garlic, peeled and crushed
1 tablespoon oil
⅔ cup dried lentils

1 teaspoon ground coriander
1 teaspoon cumin
2½ cups stock or water
1 bay leaf

Heat the oil in a fairly large saucepan and sauté the onion for 5 minutes, then add the garlic, spices and bay leaf and stir over the heat for 1–2 minutes. Put in the remaining vegetables and stir over the heat for a further 1–2 minutes so that they are all coated with the oil and spices. Add the water and a little salt and pepper. Cover and let simmer for 15–20 minutes, until the vegetables are all tender, stirring from time to time and checking to make sure they do not cook dry— there will be very little water left. Alternatively, the spiced vegetables can be put into an ovenproof casserole and baked at 325°F for about 1–1½ hours, until tender when pierced with the point of a knife.

To make the sauce, first sauté the onion and garlic in the oil for 5 minutes, until softened; then stir in the lentils and spices and cook for a further minute or two. Add the stock or water and bay leaf; bring up to the boil, then let simmer gently for 15–20 minutes, until the lentils are tender and pale gold in color. Remove the bay leaf, purée the sauce and add salt and pepper to taste.

Serve the vegetables with the sauce.

BAKED CRÊPES WITH LEEKS

This dish can be prepared in advance and then just heated through in a moderate oven when you want it. It only needs a green salad to go with it. *Serves 6–8.*

FOR THE CRÊPES:

½ cup whole-wheat flour
A pinch of sea salt
2 eggs

1 tablespoon vegetable oil
⅔ cup milk
Extra oil for cooking

FOR THE FILLING:

2 pounds leeks
1 tablespoon butter
1 tablespoon chopped fresh
  parsley

Sea salt
Freshly ground black pepper

FOR THE TOPPING:

2 eggs
⅔ cup milk

1 cup ricotta cheese
½ cup grated mozarella

First make the crêpe batter: the easiest way to do this is to put all the
ingredients into a blender or food processer and blend to a smooth,
creamy mixture. Otherwise, put the flour and salt into a bowl, break
in the eggs and beat, then gradually mix in the oil and milk to make a
smooth, creamy consistency.

To make the crêpes, brush a small skillet with a little oil and set it
over a moderate heat. When it's hot, pour in 2 tablespoons of the
batter, then tip and swirl the pan so that the mixture runs all over the
base. Then put the pan over the heat for 20–30 seconds, until the top
of the crêpe is set and the underside is flecked golden brown. Flip the
crêpe over using a small spatula and your fingers if necessary. Cook
the other side of the crêpe, then lift it out onto a plate. Brush the
skillet with more oil if necessary and make another crêpe in the same
way, putting it on top of the first one when it's done. Continue until
you have finished all the mixture and have about twelve thin crêpes.

Next make the filling. Slice and wash the leeks, then cook them in
a little fast-boiling salted water for about 10 minutes, until just tender.
Drain well and add the butter, parsley and salt and pepper to taste.

Preheat the oven to 350°F. Put a heaping tablespoon of the leek
mixture on each crêpe, roll the crêpe neatly and place it in a large,
greased, shallow casserole dish. Make the topping by quickly beating
together the eggs and milk and blending in the ricotta; season lightly
and pour this over the crêpes. Sprinkle with the grated cheese, cover the
dish with a piece of foil and bake for 40–45 minutes, removing the
foil about 15 minutes before the end of the cooking time to brown the
cheese on top.

A pleasant variation is to use a homemade tomato sauce instead of
the creamy sauce.

CHEESE FONDUE

This is a marvelous dish for those occasions when you have to make something delicious and a bit special on the spur of the moment. Because fondues are rich, I like to start with a light, fruity first course, such as pineapple wedges or melon with strawberries, and then have a refreshing salad after the fondue. If you want to serve a dessert, a tart such as the Black Currant Lattice or Bakewell Tart go well, or for something lighter, a fruit sherbert. *Serves 4–6.*

1 garlic clove
1¼ cups dry white wine
2 cups grated Gruyère cheese and
   2 cups grated Emmenthal
   cheese
1 tablespoon corn starch
1–2 tablespoons kirsch—optional

Sea salt
Freshly ground black pepper
Grated nutmeg
1 French baguette or crusty
   whole-wheat loaf—or half of
   each—cut into bite-size pieces
   and warmed in the oven

Halve the garlic and rub the cut surfaces over the inside of a medium-size saucepan (or special fondue pot). Put the wine and cheese into the saucepan and heat gently, stirring all the time until the cheese has melted. Mix the corn starch to a paste with the kirsch if you're using it, or use a drop more wine; pour this paste into the cheese mixture, stirring constantly until you have a lovely creamy consistency. Occasionally, the cheese goes all lumpy and stringy at this point. Don't despair; if you beat it vigorously for a moment or two with a hand beater, all will be well. Season the fondue, then place the saucepan over a fondue flame and let everyone start dipping their bread into the delicious mixture.

Nut Loaves and Rissoles

Although a nut or lentil loaf takes a little effort to prepare, this is more than justified by the fact that, like a meat roast, it can be served twice, first hot then cold, which saves time in the end.

I think a savory loaf needs something moist to go with it: a light puréed vegetable or a sauce, such as the Mushroom and Sour Cream Sauce (page 151) or fresh Tomato Sauce (page 153). A chilled yoghurt and herb dressing or mayonnaise goes well with cold, sliced nut or lentil loaf and, thinly sliced, these are also good as fillings for sandwiches or rolls.

The burgers are also good in fresh light rolls or French bread, especially if they're cooked and eaten sizzling hot out-of-doors, with plenty of good mustard and salad to go with them.

All the nut loaves freeze well, either before or after baking, though I think partial baking for about 30 minutes before freezing gives the best results. The burgers are best frozen uncovered on a baking sheet, if you have the space in your freezer, then packed in a plastic bag. You can then cook them frozen.

CHESTNUT SAGE AND RED WINE LOAF

This is a moist, savory loaf that slices well either hot or cold. Served with baked red cabbage and baked potatoes with sour cream, it makes a very pleasant winter meal. This loaf is also very good as a vegetarian alternative to Christmas turkey, with Special Wine Sauce, Bread Sauce, roast potatoes and baby Brussels sprouts. *Serves 6.*

Butter and dry bread crumbs for lining loaf pan
2¼ pounds fresh chestnuts
1 large onion, peeled and chopped
2 celery stalks, finely chopped
4 tablespoons butter or polyunsaturated margarine
2 garlic cloves, peeled and crushed

2 tablespoons chopped fresh sage or 1 teaspoon dried
1 tablespoon dry red wine
1 egg
Sea salt
Freshly ground black pepper
1 fresh sage leaf if available, for garnish

Preheat the oven to 350°F. Prepare an 8 x 4-inch loaf pan by lining the bottom and narrow sides with a long strip of waxed paper or cooking parchment; brush well with butter and sprinkle lightly with the dry bread crumbs.

Make a slit in each chestnut with a knife, then simmer in plenty of water for about 10 minutes, until the slits open. Take the chestnuts from the water one by one and peel off the skins with a sharp, pointed knife. Put the peeled chestnuts into a saucepan, cover with water and simmer for 20–30 minutes, until tender. Drain and mash the chestnuts.

Melt the butter or margarine in a large saucepan and sauté the onion and celery for 10 minutes, without browning. Add the chestnuts, garlic, sage, wine and egg and mix together, seasoning with salt and pepper.

Lay the sage leaf, if available, in the bottom of the prepared loaf pan and spoon the chestnut mixture on top. Smooth over the surface and cover with a piece of foil. Bake the loaf in the preheated oven for 1 hour. To serve, slip a knife around the sides of the loaf and turn out onto a warm serving dish.

LENTIL, HAZELNUT AND CIDER LOAF

The cider gives this loaf a lovely rich, fruity flavor, though you can leave it out and use a good vegetable stock if you prefer, or try a cheapish red wine instead, which is also delicious—and better if you want to drink red wine with the meal. The loaf is rich in protein and very good hot, perhaps with fresh Tomato Sauce and Potatoes with Lemon; or cold, with salad and homemade mayonnaise. It can also be used as a sandwich filling, cut into thin slices and spread with mild mustard or chutney. *Serves 6–8.*

1 cup dried lentils
2 cups apple cider
Butter and dry bread crumbs for
    lining loaf pan
1 large onion, peeled and chopped
1 large carrot, scraped and
    chopped
1 celery stalk, chopped
1 garlic clove, peeled and crushed
2 tablespoons butter

1 teaspoon dried thyme
½ cup hazelnuts
½ cup grated Swiss cheese
1 tablespoon chopped fresh
    parsley
1 egg
Sea salt
Freshly ground black pepper
Parsley springs, for garnish

Put the lentils and cider into a saucepan and bring to the boil; turn the heat down, half cover the saucepan and let simmer over a fairly low heat for 20 minutes, until the lentils are tender and all the water is absorbed.

When the lentils are nearly cooked, preheat the oven to 350°F. Prepare an 8 x 4-inch loaf pan by lining the bottom and narrow sides with a long strip of waxed paper, or cooking parchment; brush well with butter and sprinkle lightly with dry bread crumbs. Next, sauté the onion, carrot, celery and garlic in the butter for 10 minutes, until they are softened and lightly browned. Add the sautéed vegetables to the lentils, together with the thyme, nuts, cheese, parsley and egg. Mix everything together thoroughly and add salt and plenty of pepper to taste.

Spoon the mixture into the prepared pan, smooth over the surface and cover with a piece of foil. Bake the loaf in the preheated oven for

1 hour, then remove the foil and cook for a further 10–15 minutes to brown the top. To serve, slip a knife around the sides of the loaf and turn out onto a warm serving dish. Decorate the top with some sprigs of fresh green parsley.

PINE-NUT LOAF WITH HERB STUFFING

This dish consists of two layers of moist, delicately flavored, pine nuts with a layer of green herb stuffing in the middle. It's a favorite vegetarian alternative to Christmas turkey and popular with my family at any time. The pine nuts are expensive and, though lovely for a special occasion, can be replaced by cheaper nuts, such as cashews or almonds. I would serve this loaf with golden roast potatoes and either wine sauce and a lightly cooked green vegetable or the Purée of Brussels Sprouts (page 86); the Apple and Cranberry Sauce (page 149) also goes very well with this loaf. *Serves 6.*

Butter and dry bread crumbs for
    lining loaf pan
1 onion, peeled and chopped
2 tablespoons butter
½ pound pine nuts or a mixture
    of pine nuts, almonds and
    cashews, finely chopped

4 tablespoons milk
2 cups soft, white bread crumbs
2 eggs
Sea salt
Freshly ground black pepper
Grated nutmeg

FOR THE STUFFING:

3 cups soft whole-wheat bread
    crumbs
½ cup butter
Grated rind and juice of ½
    small lemon

½ teaspoon dried marjoram
½ teaspoon dried thyme
4 heaping tablespoons chopped
    fresh parsley

TO FINISH:

2 tablespoons pine nuts, lightly
    roasted

Parsley sprigs
Lemon slices

Preheat the oven to 350°F. Line an 8 x 4-inch loaf pan with a long strip of waxed paper, or cooking parchment to cover the narrow sides and bottom of the pan; grease very well with butter and sprinkle with dry bread crumbs—this helps the loaf to come out of the pan cleanly. Melt the butter in a medium-size saucepan and sauté the onion for 10 minutes, until soft but not browned. Take the saucepan off the heat and mix in the rest of the ingredients, seasoning well with salt, pepper and grated nutmeg. Next make the stuffing by mixing all the ingredients together and seasoning well.

To assemble the loaf, first spoon half the nut mixture into the prepared pan. Then, with your hands, press the stuffing mixture into a rectangle the right size to make a layer on top of the nut mixture; put it gently in place and spoon the rest of the nut mixture on top. Smooth the surface, cover with a piece of buttered foil and bake for 1 hour.

Remove the foil and have a look at the nut loaf; if you think it needs to be a bit browner on top, pop it back into the oven, uncovered, for a further 5–10 minutes. If possible, let the loaf stand for 3–4 minutes after you take it out of the oven—this helps it to "settle" and come out of the pan more easily. Then slip a knife down the sides of the loaf, turn it out of the pan onto a warmed serving dish and strip off the piece of paper. Garnish with the roasted nuts, parsley and lemon.

WHITE NUT LOAF WITH CAPERS

My original idea with this recipe was to use green peppercorns; when it was sliced I wanted to get the effect of white flecked with green. But the number of peppercorns necessary for that made the loaf far too hot! So then I hit on the idea of using capers instead, and I must say I was very pleased with the result: the slices look just as I envisioned them and the capers give the loaf a lovely tangy flavor. The loaf is good served hot with a rich sauce—Béarnaise is lovely—or cold, with mayonnaise and salad. *Serves 6.*

Butter and dry bread crumbs for
    lining loaf pan
1 onion, peeled and chopped
2 tablespoons butter
½ pound cashews, or half cashews
    and half almonds, finely
    chopped

¼ cup milk
2 cups soft white bread crumbs
2 eggs
Sea salt
Freshly ground black pepper
2 jars (2 ounces each) capers,
    drained

TO FINISH:

A few extra capers and whole
    cashews, lightly roasted

Preheat the oven to 350°F. Line an 8 x 4-inch loaf pan with a long strip
of waxed paper or cooking parchment to cover the narrow sides and
bottom of the pan; grease very well with butter and sprinkle with dry
bread crumbs—this helps the loaf to come out of the pan cleanly. Melt
the butter in a medium-size saucepan and sauté the onion for 10
minutes, until soft but not browned. Take the saucepan off the heat
and mix in the nuts, milk, bread crumbs, egg and a good seasoning of
salt and pepper. Gently fold in the capers, being careful not to mash
them.

Spoon the mixture into the prepared pan, smooth the surface, cover
with a piece of buttered foil and bake for 1 hour.

Remove the foil and have a look at the nut loaf; if you think it
needs to be a bit browner on top, pop it back into the oven, uncovered,
for a further 5–10 minutes. If possible, let the loaf stand for 3–4
minutes after you take it out of the oven—this helps it to "settle" and
come out of the pan more easily. Then slip a knife down the sides
of the loaf, turn it out into a warmed serving dish and strip off the
piece of paper.

Decorate with a row of capers down the center and some roasted
cashews on either side.

WHITE NUT RISSOLES BAKED
WITH MUSHROOMS

In this recipe, light, delicately flavored nut rissoles are baked on a moist base of fried mushrooms and onions. They're delicious with a light vegetable dish or fluffy brown rice and a green salad. *Serves 3–4.*

FOR THE SAUCE:

1 tablespoon butter
1 tablespoon oil
1 large onion, peeled and chopped
2 garlic cloves, peeled and crushed

½ pound mushrooms, washed and sliced
2 tablespoons dry white wine
2 tablespoons light cream— optional

FOR THE NUT RISSOLES:

1 cup finely chopped cashews
1 cup soft white bread crumbs
½ cup grated Swiss cheese
1 egg

½ teaspoon dried thyme
Sea salt
Freshly ground black pepper
Fresh parsley, chopped

First prepare the mushroom mixture. Heat the butter and oil in a medium-size saucepan and sauté the onion for 5 minutes, until it begins to soften; then add the garlic and mushrooms and sauté for a further 5 minutes. Add the wine, let the mixture bubble and scrape down the crusty bits from the sides of the pan. Remove from the heat and season to taste. Pour the mixture into a shallow casserole dish.

Preheat the oven to 350°F. Make the rissoles by mixing all the ingredients together; season with salt and plenty of pepper. Form the mixture into eight rissoles, or small balls, and put them on top of the mushroom mixture. Bake, uncovered, for 25–30 minutes, until the rissoles are puffed up a little and are firm but not hard. Pour the cream into the casserole dish, around the rissoles, sprinkle with chopped parsley and serve.

A pleasant variation is to put a cooked chestnut (or a well-drained canned chestnut) into the center of each nut rissole, molding the white nut mixture gently around it.

BROWN NUT RISSOLES IN TOMATO SAUCE

This is really a variation of the previous recipe, but using brown nuts and whole-wheat bread crumbs for the rissoles and baking them in a fresh-tasting tomato sauce produces quite a different effect. These are delicious served with buttery whole-wheat spaghetti, Parmesan cheese and a crisp green salad with a good olive oil dressing. *Serves 3–4.*

FOR THE SAUCE:

1 tablespoon oil
1 onion, peeled and chopped
1 clove garlic, peeled and crushed

1 pound tomatoes, peeled and
    chopped, or use 1 can (16
    ounces)
Sea salt
Freshly ground black pepper

FOR THE NUT RISSOLES:

1 small onion, chopped
1 tablespoon butter
1 cup brown nuts such as
    unblanched almonds or
    roasted hazelnuts—see
    page 22
1 cup soft whole-wheat
    bread crumbs

1½ cups Cheddar cheese,
    finely grated
2 heaping teaspoons tomato paste
1 egg
½ teaspoon dried thyme
Sea salt
Freshly ground black pepper

Start by making the sauce. Heat the oil in a medium-size saucepan and sauté the onion for 10 minutes, until softened but not browned. Add the garlic and tomatoes, and cook for a further 15 minutes, until the tomatoes have collapsed and reduced to a thick consistency. Purée the mixture and season with salt and pepper.

Next, preheat the oven to 350°F. Sauté the onion in the butter and make the rissoles by simply mixing all the ingredients together and seasoning to taste. Form the mixture into eight rissoles, or small balls, and place them in a greased shallow ovenproof dish. Pour the sauce over the rissoles and bake them in the preheated oven for 25–30 minutes, until they are puffy but firm to the touch.

NUT RISSOLES IN RATATOUILLE

Another variation is to bake the nut rissoles, either the white or brown version, in ratatouille. Prepare and cook the Ratatouille, as described on page 96, and put it into a shallow ovenproof dish; put the nut rissoles on top of the ratatouille and bake as described for Nut Rissoles in Tomato Sauce, page 127.

VEGETARIAN SCOTCH EGGS

Scotch eggs look attractive when they're sliced, and are ideal for picnics and buffets. The secret of getting the coating to stick to the egg is to dip the hard-boiled egg into beaten egg beforehand. The protein content of these Scotch eggs is excellent, and they're good for lunch boxes, with a nice crisp salad. *Makes 4.*

1 onion, peeled and grated
½ cup finely roasted hazelnuts, chopped
½ cup finely chopped almonds
½ cup grated Parmesan cheese
2 teaspoons tomato paste
1 egg
1 tablespoon chopped fresh thyme, or 1 teaspoon dried

1 tablespoon vegetarian stock or water
Sea salt
Freshly ground black pepper
4 hard-boiled eggs, shelled
Beaten egg and crisp whole-wheat crumbs to coat
Fat for deep-frying

First make the coating for the Scotch eggs; simply mix the onion, nuts, cheese, tomato, egg and thyme together to make a fairly firm paste and season, adding the stock or water to soften the consistency a little, if necessary.

To finish the eggs, dip the whole hard-boiled eggs into the beaten egg and then roll them in the nut mixture to cover them completely. Coat the Scotch eggs in egg and bread crumbs. Heat the oil in a deep skillet to a temperature of 375°F, then deep-fry the Scotch eggs for 2–3 minutes, until golden brown and crisp, and drain on paper toweling. Leave the Scotch eggs until they are cool, then cut each in half or into quarters and serve with salad.

Pies, Quiches, Pizzas and Pasta

Vegetable pies, quiches and pizzas are so useful, being substantial yet easy to eat and versatile enough to be served hot or cold, on their own or as part of a meal, with sauces and hot vegetables or salads.

If they are made with whole-wheat flour, they are also healthy and nutritious, good for everyday fare as well as special occasions. They're fairly high in fat, however, so they're best when served with fairly plain cooked vegetables or salads without too much oil, followed by a fresh fruit dessert.

Again, for health reasons, I like to use polyunsaturated margarine where I can in cooking, and I do find you can make a very good, light, whole-wheat shortcrust pastry with it. I use that for most quiches and tarts, but the flaky pastry I like to make as a treat for special occasions does require a hard fat and for this I use well-chilled butter.

ASPARAGUS QUICHE

This is a creamy, delicious quiche with a crisp pastry shell. You could use all cream, if you like, but I find this lighter mixture of cream and sour cream works well. This is lovely for an early summer lunch, with buttered new potatoes. *Serves 6.*

FOR THE PASTRY:

1½ cups whole-wheat flour   *1½ tablespoons cold water*
6 tablespoons polyunsaturated
 margarine or butter

FOR THE FILLING:

1 pound fresh or frozen asparagus   *1 cup grated Cheddar cheese*
Sea salt   *⅔ cup light cream*
Freshly ground black pepper   *½ cup sour cream*
2 tablespoons oil   *2 eggs*
1 small onion, peeled and chopped   *Fresh parsley, chopped*

First cook the asparagus for the filling. If you're using fresh asparagus, break off the hard stems—these ends are too tough to eat but can be used to make a stock for asparagus soup. Wash the asparagus gently to remove any grit, then place in a steamer and cook for about 10 minutes, until just tender when pierced with a pointed knife. Cook frozen asparagus according to the directions on the package. Drain and season with salt and pepper.

To make the pastry, sift the flour into a large bowl and just tip in the bran left in the sieve. Rub the margarine or butter into the flour, using a pastry blender or a fork, until the mixture resembles fine bread crumbs. Add the cold water and press the mixture together to form a dough. If there's time leave the dough to rest for 30 minutes (this makes it easier to roll out but isn't essential). Preheat the oven to 400°F, and, if possible, place a heavy baking sheet on the top shelf to heat up with the oven. Roll out the pastry and ease it into an 8-inch lightly greased quiche/tart pan. Trim the edges and prick the base. Put the pastry shell into the oven on top of the baking sheet and bake for 15 minutes, until the pastry is lightly browned and firm to the touch.

While the pastry is in the oven, heat the oil in a large saucepan and sauté the onion for 10 minutes, until the onion has softened and lightly browned. Have the onion piping hot when you take the pastry shell out of the oven and pour this, oil and all, over the bottom of the shell. This makes the pastry crisp (and ensures that it will stay crisp after the filling is added). At this juncture, the pastry shell and onion can be left to cool and the rest of the filling added later if more convenient.

To finish the quiche, reduce the oven setting to 350°F. Arrange the cooked asparagus over the onion and sprinkle with half the cheese. Beat the cream, sour cream and eggs together until smooth; season with salt and freshly ground black pepper. Pour this mixture over the onion, asparagus and cheese and sprinkle with the remaining cheese. Bake for 30 minutes, until the filling is puffed up, golden and set. Sprinkle with chopped parsley before serving.

EGGPLANT, RED PEPPER AND CHEESE QUICHE

This is a pretty quiche, its chunky eggplant filling set in a light custard. I think the nutty flavor of the whole-wheat pastry goes well with the onion and eggplant filling. This is best served hot, with buttered new potatoes and green beans. *Serves 6.*

FOR THE PASTRY:

1½ cups whole-wheat flour
6 tablespoons polyunsaturated
   margarine or butter

1½ tablespoons cold water

FOR THE FILLING:

1 medium-size eggplant
3 tablespoons oil
2 large onions, peeled and
   chopped
1 red pepper
1 fat clove of garlic, peeled and
   crushed in a little salt

Sea salt
Freshly ground black pepper
1 cup grated Cheddar cheese
2 eggs
¾ cup milk

First prepare the eggplant. Wash the eggplant and remove the stem, then cut it into ½-inch cubes. Put these into a colander, sprinkle them with salt and then place a plate and a weight on top and let stand for at least 30 minutes. Rinse the pieces of eggplant under cold water and blot with paper towels to remove excess water.

Preheat the oven to 400°F. Make the pastry shell as described for the Asparagus Quiche, page 130, and bake for 15 minutes.

While the pastry shell is in the oven, heat 2 tablespoons of the oil in a large saucepan and sauté the onion for 10 minutes, until softened and lightly browned. Have the sautéed onion piping hot when you take the pastry out of the oven and pour this, oil and all, over the bottom of the hot shell.

To finish, reduce the oven setting to 350°F. Heat the remaining tablespoon of oil in a medium-size saucepan and sauté the eggplant, red pepper and garlic for about 10 minutes, until they are tender but not too soft. Season with salt and freshly ground black pepper. Sprinkle two-thirds of the grated cheese over the onion in the shell, then spoon the eggplant mixture on top and sprinkle with the rest of the cheese. Beat the eggs and milk together and pour evenly over the vegetables and cheese. Bake in the top third of the oven for 50–60 minutes, until the filling is set and golden.

CAULIFLOWER, STILTON AND WALNUT QUICHE

This quiche consists of a crisp whole-wheat pastry with a filling of cauliflower with Stilton cheese and walnuts. Serve with a crisp salad and new potatoes with parsley for a more substantial meal. *Serves 6.*

FOR THE PASTRY:

1½ cups whole-wheat flour
6 tablespoons polyunsaturated
  margarine or butter

1½ tablespoons cold water

FOR THE FILLING:

1 medium-size cauliflower—about
   1 pound trimmed
Sea salt
Freshly ground black pepper
1 cup grated or crumbled Stilton
   cheese

½ cup coarsley chopped walnuts
2 eggs
¾ cup milk

Preheat the oven to 400°F. Make the pastry shell as described for the Asparagus Quiche (page 130), and bake for 15 minutes. Lower the oven setting to 375°F.

While the pastry is baking, make the filling. Break the cauliflower into florets, then slice these so that they will lie fairly flat in the pastry shell. Cook the cauliflower in 1-inch of fast-boiling lightly salted water for 5 minutes, until just barely tender when pierced with the point of a knife. Drain well and season with salt and pepper.

Scatter two-thirds of the cheese and half the walnuts in the bottom of the pastry shell, then arrange the cauliflower so that it's just about level with the top of the shell, and sprinkle with the rest of the cheese and walnuts. Beat the eggs and milk and pour evenly over the top of the vegetable mixture. Bake in the top third of the oven for 50–60 minutes, until the filling is set. Serve at once, if possible.

DEEP-DISH MUSHROOM PIE

My aim with this was to make a pie that could be cut into slices for a party or buffet. It looks very attractive, especially if you can make it in a long, thin loaf pan. I have one with collapsible sides that is 3 inches deep with an inside base measurment of 9¾ x 3¼ inches and a top measurement of 10¾ x 4¼ inches, and that is ideal, but the capacity is the same as that of a standard 9 x 5-inch loaf pan, so you can use that instead, lined with greased foil to help ease the pie out after baking. *Serves 10.*

3 cups whole-wheat flour   Beaten egg, for glaze
Salt
1 cup polyunsaturated
   margarine

FOR THE FILLING:

2 tablespoons butter   2 eggs, beaten
1 large onion, peeled and chopped 1 tablespoon lemon juice
2 large garlic cloves, peeled and 3 tablespoons chopped fresh
   crushed   parsley
¾ pound fresh mushrooms   1 teaspoon ground mace
2 cups finely chopped almonds   Freshly ground black pepper
1 cup grated Swiss cheese   3 or 4 hard-boiled eggs

First make the pastry. Sift the flour into a large bowl with a little salt, and just tip in the bran that will be left in the sieve. Rub the margarine into the flour—a pastry blender or fork is easiest for this—then press the mixture together to form a dough. If there's time refrigerate this dough for 30 minutes (this makes it easier to roll out but isn't essential).

Meanwhile make the filling. Melt the butter in a large saucepan and sauté the onion for 10 minutes, until soft but not browned; add the garlic and sauté for a further minute or two. Then take the saucepan off the heat and stir in all the remaining ingredients except the hard-boiled eggs. Season with salt and pepper.

Preheat the oven to 400°F, and if possible place a heavy baking sheet on the top shelf to heat up with the oven. Roll out three-quarters of the pastry and ease it into the loaf pan, which has been well greased if it's a collapsible one or lined with well-greased foil if not. This is not an easy process since the pastry is fragile, and I find it usually breaks and has to be pieced together—this doesn't matter; just patch it up and press it together. Spoon in half the filling, then put the hard-boiled eggs on top. Cover with the remaining mixture. Roll the last piece of pastry into a rectangle to fit the top of the pie and press into position. Trim the edges, decorate with the pastry trimmings, brush with beaten egg and make several holes in the top to allow the steam to escape.

Bake the pie for 30 minutes, then turn the oven setting down to 350°F, and bake for a further 30 minutes. Leave the pie to cool in the pan, then remove it carefully. It slices best when chilled a little.

DEEP-DISH VEGETABLE PIE

This idea came to me when I was telling a friend about the Deep-Dish Mushroom Pie (page 134), and she suggested I try a variation of a Cornish pasty, which is traditionally made from root vegetables and does not contain meat. So I used the same deep loaf pan and, so that the pie would look good when sliced, I layered the thinly sliced vegetables. I was very pleased with the result; the pie looks good and slices well. Other variations are possible: you can add thin layers of different colored grated cheeses, or chopped parsley to make a green layer. It's delicious served hot with Yoghurt and Scallion Sauce or Lemon Mayonnaise. *Serves 10.*

FOR THE PASTRY:

3 cups whole-wheat flour
1 cup polyunsaturated margarine

Beaten egg, for glaze

FOR THE FILLING:

½ pound turnip or parsnip,
   peeled
1 pound carrots, scraped
½ pound potatoes, peeled

Sea salt
Freshly ground black pepper
Grated nutmeg

First make the pastry as described for the Deep-Dish Mushroom Pie (page 134) and refrigerate it while you prepare the filling.

Slice the vegetables as thinly as possible, preferably in a food processor. Keep the different types separate, covered with water if necessary, until you're ready to use them.

Preheat the oven to 400°F. Roll out the pastry and line the loaf pan as described in the earlier recipe. Put the sliced turnip or parsnip in an even layer in the pie, pressing down well. Season to taste with salt, pepper and grated nutmeg. Follow this with a layer of half the carrot, then the potato, followed by the rest of the carrot, seasoning each layer as you go.

Roll the last piece of pastry into a rectangle to fit the top of the pie and press into position. Trim the edges, decorate with the pastry trimmings, brush with the beaten egg and make several holes in the top to allow the steam to escape. Bake the pie for 30 minutes then turn the oven setting down to 325°F, and bake for another hour, covering the pastry with foil for the last half hour or so if it is getting too brown. Remove the pie from the pan and serve hot; or, if you are going to serve it cold, let it cool in the pan, then remove it carefully. I like it best hot.

FLAKY MUSHROOM ROLL

This is a lovely flaky, golden pastry roll with a moist mushroom filling. The pastry isn't difficult to make but you need to allow time for it to chill in the fridge before baking. *Serves 6.*

FOR THE PASTRY:

1 cup chilled butter
½ cup ice-cold water
A few drops of lemon juice

2 cups whole-wheat flour
Beaten egg, for glaze

FOR THE FILLING:

2 tablespoons butter or
polyunsaturated margarine
1 onion, peeled and chopped
1 large clove garlic, peeled and
crushed
1 pound fresh mushrooms, wiped
and chopped
2 tablespoons chopped fresh
parsley

2 hard-boiled eggs, chopped—
optional
2 cups cooked brown rice
½ teaspoon powdered mace
Sea salt
Freshly ground black pepper

First make the pastry. Make sure that the butter is really hard and the water as cold as possible. It's a good idea to put the flour into a large bowl and chill that, too, if you can. One of the secrets of success with this pastry is to have everything, including your hands, as cool as possible.

Cut the butter into small pieces with the flour and mix lightly. Add the water and lemon juice and mix gently with a metal spoon to make a loose, lumpy dough.

Put the dough on a well-floured board and turn it once or twice in the flour. Then, using light strokes, roll it out into a long oblong. Fold the top third of the oblong down and the bottom third up so that you have three layers. Half turn the block of pastry and repeat this four times in all. Wrap the dough in waxed paper and refrigerate for at least two hours before using it.

Melt the butter or margarine in a large pan and sauté the onion for a few minutes, until soft and transparent but not browned. Add the garlic and mushrooms and cook over a low heat until most of the moisture given off by the mushrooms has evaporated. (If too much moisture is left in the pan at this stage, the mixture will make the pastry soggy later on.) Stir in the parsley, eggs and rice. Season with the mace and salt and pepper to taste. Set to one side while you finish preparing the pastry, which has been chilling in the fridge.

To assemble and finish the roll, set the oven to 425°F. Sprinkle a little flour on a pastry board and roll the pastry into a square about 12 x 12 inches. Heap the mushroom mixture in the center of the pastry and wrap the pastry over it, moistening the edges with a little cold water and pressing them together to seal and make a neat oblong. Place this, seam side down, on a baking sheet; roll out the pastry trimmings and cut out a few leaves to garnish the roll. Make one or two cuts or holes in the top to allow the steam to escape, brush with beaten egg and bake in the top third of the oven for 30 minutes, then turn the heat down to 375°F, for a further 25–30 minutes. This is nice with the Yoghurt and Fresh Herb Sauce (page 152), made with fennel if available, and a green salad.

MUSHROOM PUDDING

This is a steamed pudding, rather like a vegetarian steak and kidney pudding. It's very easy to do and makes a warming meal in winter. I like to serve it with mashed potatoes and the Red Cabbage with Apples Baked in Cider on page 88. *Serves 4.*

FOR THE PASTRY:

1½ cups whole-wheat flour
6 tablespoons polyunsaturated
   margarine

1 cup grated Parmesan cheese
2 tablespoons water

FOR THE FILLING:

¾ pound fresh mushrooms, wiped
   and sliced
1 onion, peeled and chopped
1 teaspoon tomato paste
1 small clove garlic, peeled and
   crushed

Sea salt
Freshly ground black pepper
1 teaspoon yeast extract
   (Marmite)
2 tablespoons hot water

First make the pastry. Sift the flour into a large bowl, and just tip in the bran left in the sieve. Rub the margarine into the flour using a pastry blender or a fork until the mixture resembles fine bread crumbs. Add the cheese and water and press the mixture together to form a dough. If there's time, refrigerate the dough for 30 minutes (this makes it easier to roll out but isn't essential). Grease a 1-quart steamed-pudding mold.

To make the filling, put the mushrooms into a bowl and mix with the remaining ingredients, softening the yeast extract in the hot water. Roll out two-thirds of the pastry and use to line the pudding mold; spoon the mushroom mixture into the pastry, then cover with the rest of the pastry, rolled out to fit the top. Trim the edges and prick the top with a fork. Cover with the mold's lid, or a piece of foil, secured with string. Steam the pudding for 2½ hours. When it's done, slip a knife down the sides to loosen the pudding, then turn it out onto a warmed serving dish.

WALNUT PÂTE EN CROÛTE

This makes a delicious main course for a special meal: a moist wine-flavored nut pâté in a crisp crust of golden pastry. The quantities I've given here make a handsome dish that will feed 12 easily. If you think this is too much, the amounts can simply be halved; but the pâté is also delicious cold and will freeze well before cooking. Just as for the Flaky Mushroom Roll (page 137), remember to chill the pastry before baking. I try to make it the night before I need it, if possible. *Serves 12.*

FOR THE FLAKY PASTRY:

1 cup chilled butter
½ cup ice-cold water

A few drops of lemon juice
2 cups whole-wheat flour

FOR THE NUT PÂTÉ:

2 tablespoons butter
1 large onion, peeled and chopped
1 stalk of celery, finely chopped
2 large garlic cloves, peeled and crushed
1 cup ground walnuts
2½ cups ground cashews
1 cup chestnut purée
1 cup grated Cheddar cheese

2 eggs
2 tablespoons brandy
½ teaspoon paprika
½ teaspoon dried thyme
Sea salt
Freshly ground black pepper
½ pound mushrooms, washed
Beaten egg, for glaze

First make the pastry as described for the Flaky Mushroom Roll on page 137. You need to do this an hour or so in advance to give it a chance to chill before you use it.

While the pastry is chilling, make the nut pâté. Melt the butter in a medium-size saucepan and sauté the onion and celery for 10 minutes, until soft but not browned. Remove from the heat and stir in the garlic, nuts, cheese, eggs, brandy, paprika, thyme and salt and pepper seasoning to taste.

To assemble and finish the pâté, preheat the oven to 425°F. Sprinkle a little flour on a pastry board and roll the fold of pastry into a rectangle about 12 x 16 inches. Spoon the pâté in the center of the pastry and place the mushrooms on top. Brush the edges of the pastry with a little cold water, then fold them over to enclose the pâté and mush-rooms completely but not too tightly, to allow for the pâté to expand a little as it cooks. Place the pastry parcel seam side down on a baking sheet; roll out the pastry trimmings and cut out some leaves to garnish the roll. Make one or two cuts or holes in the top to allow the steam to escape, brush with beaten egg and bake in the top third of the oven for 30 minutes; then turn the heat down to 375°F, for a further 25–30 minutes. I like to serve this with a purée of Brussels sprouts and new potatoes with butter and chopped parsley; the Mushroom and Sour-Cream Sauce on page 151 also goes well with it.

SPECIAL PIZZA

A pizza isn't nearly as difficult to make as many people think, and it's one of the most delicious vegetarian dishes. This recipe takes about 2½ hours to make from start to finish, but during most of that time the dough is rising, so you're not tied to the kitchen. *Serves 4–8: Makes 4 8-inch or 2 12-inch pizzas.*

FOR THE CRUST:

1 package active dry yeast
1 teaspoon sugar
1 cup warm water
3½ cups whole-wheat flour

2 teaspoons salt
2 tablespoons soft butter or vegetable margarine
1 large egg, beaten

FOR THE TOPPING:

2 tablespoons olive oil
2 large onions, peeled and chopped
1 clove garlic, crushed
¼ pound button mushrooms, wiped and sliced
1 can (29 ounces) tomatoes, drained
Sea salt

Freshly ground black pepper
4–6 canned artichoke hearts, sliced
1 medium sweet red pepper, cut into slices
2 cups grated Mozarella cheese
A few black olives, pitted
2 teaspoons oregano
Olive oil

Dissolve the yeast and sugar in ¼ cup of the water. Let stand for 10 minutes, until the yeast is foamy.

Put the flour and salt into a large bowl and work in the butter or margarine with a pastry blender or a fork. Make a well in the center and pour in the yeast mixture, the rest of the water and the beaten egg. Mix to a firm dough, which will leave the sides of the bowl clean—add a tiny bit more flour or water if necessary to achieve this. Turn the dough out onto a clean working surface and knead for 10 minutes, until the texture becomes smooth and pliable. Then place the dough back in a greased bowl, cover the bowl and leave in a warm place until the dough has doubled in size—about 1½ hours.

Preheat the oven to 400°F. Take the dough out of the bowl and punch it down to remove any large pockets of air. Knead for 2 minutes, then divide the dough into two or four pieces and roll each into a 12-inch or 8-inch circle. These can be put onto large ovenproof pizza plates or well-greased baking sheets, whichever is most convenient.

It's best to make the filling while the dough is rising for the first time. Heat the oil in a medium-size saucepan and sauté the onion and garlic for 10 minutes, until softened; then add the mushrooms and cook for a further 2–3 minutes. Remove from the heat, stir in the tomatoes (chopping them up with a spoon) and season to taste.

Spoon the tomato mixture on top of the pizzas, dividing it evenly among them. Arrange the artichoke hearts, red pepper strips, cheese and olives on top; sprinkle with oregano and a little olive oil. Let rise for 30 minutes.

Bake the pizzas for about 20 minutes, until the topping is bubbling and the bread puffed up and lightly browned. Serve at once, with a good green salad and red wine.

INDIVIDUAL PIZZAS

I find it very handy to keep a few small pizzas on hand in the freezer, ready to be heated up quickly when people come in at odd times for meals. This recipe will make eight such pizzas: divide the mixture into eight pieces instead of four and roll each into a circle about 4 inches across. Complete each with the topping, as described above, let rise, bake and then open-freeze the pizzas. When they're frozen they can be packed in a plastic bag and used one by one as required. They can be cooked in a skillet and finished off under the broiler, and take about 15 minutes from frozen. When I'm feeling ambitious I make a double batch (twice the quantities given above) and stock up the freezer—but they don't last long!

LENTIL LASAGNE

This dish consists of layers of lasagne and a tasty mixture of lentils, tomatoes and wine, topped with a cheese sauce. I must admit that, contrary to my whole-food principles, I prefer this dish made with egg lasagne rather than with the whole-wheat type, although it works with either. If you use egg lasagne, you can add fiber with a final topping of whole-wheat bread crumbs mixed with a tablespoon of fine bran. The lasagne can be made in advance and only needs a crisp green salad and perhaps some red wine to go with it. *Serves 4–6.*

1 onion, peeled and chopped
2 tablespoons oil
2 garlic cloves, peeled and crushed
1 medium-large red or green
  pepper, seeded and chopped
1 cup dried lentils
1 can (15 ounces) tomatoes
1 bay leaf
1¼ cups vegetable stock or water
2 tablespoons tomato paste
⅔ cup dry red wine
¼ teaspoon each of dried oregano,
  thyme and basil

½ teaspoon cinnamon
1 tablespoon butter
1 tablespoon chopped parsley
Sea salt
Freshly ground black pepper
Sugar
1 package (8 ounces) lasagne

FOR THE TOPPING:
2 eggs
⅔ cup milk
1 cup ricotta cheese
½ cup grated Parmesan cheese

Heat the oil in a medium-size saucepan and sauté the onion for 10 minutes, then add the garlic, pepper, lentils, tomatoes, bay leaf, stock or water and tomato paste. Bring to the boil and simmer gently for 20–30 minutes, until the lentils are tender and most of the water absorbed. Remove bay leaf, and stir in the wine, herbs, cinnamon, butter and chopped parsley. Mix well, then add salt, pepper and a little sugar to taste.

While the lentil mixture is cooking, prepare the lasagne. Fill a large saucepan with lightly salted water and bring to the boil. Ease the pieces of lasagne into the boiling water and cook them for about 8 minutes, until they are just tender, then drain and drape the pieces of lasagne around the edge of the colander so they don't stick together.

Preheat the oven to 400°F. Put a layer of lasagne in the base of a shallow ovenproof dish and cover with half the lentil mixture; follow this with another layer of lasagne, followed by the rest of the lentil mixture, finishing with a layer of lasagne. Beat together the eggs and milk and blend into ricotta; season lightly and spread this over the top. Sprinkle with the grated cheese. Bake for about 45 minutes, until golden brown and bubbling.

Lentil Lasagne freezes very well, without the topping.

SPAGHETTI WITH LENTIL AND WINE SAUCE

This is a delicious spaghetti dish with a rich-tasting lentil and tomato sauce. The protein in the spaghetti complements that of the lentils, with a bit more from the cheese besides, so this dish is very nourishing. The lentil sauce can be made in advance, if convenient, and reheated when you need it. Serve with a robust red wine and a green salad with a good garlicky dressing, and finish with fruit or a good cheese—or ice cream if you're in the mood and want to keep the Italian theme—for a lovely, inexpensive and comforting meal. *Serves 3–4.*

1 tablespoon olive oil
1 onion, peeled and chopped
1 large clove garlic, peeled and
    crushed
1 teaspoon chopped basil
½ pound tomatoes, peeled and
    chopped—or use 1 can (8
    ounces) drained
½ cup dried lentils

1 tablespoon tomato paste
1¼ cups dry red wine
1¼ cups vegetable stock or water
Sea salt
Freshly ground black pepper
1 box (8 ounces) spaghetti
Butter
Grated Parmesan cheese

Heat the oil in a medium-size saucepan and sauté the onion for 10 minutes, until softened and lightly browned. Add the garlic, basil, tomatoes, lentils, tomato paste, wine and stock. Bring to the boil, then put a lid on the saucepan, turn down the heat and leave to cook gently for about 45 minutes, stirring from time to time, until the lentils are tender and the mixture is reduced to a thick purée. Season with sea salt and plenty of freshly ground black pepper. Just before the lentil mixture is done, cook the spaghetti in a large saucepan of boiling salted water, drain well, return the spaghetti to the hot saucepan with a knob of butter and toss the spaghetti so that it is coated with the melted butter and looks glossy and appetizing. Put the spaghetti on a large, heated serving dish, pour the lentil sauce on top and sprinkle with grated Parmesan cheese.

Sauces and Salad Dressings

Apple and Cranberry Sauce

Bread Sauce

Special Wine Sauce

Mushroom and Sour-Cream Sauce

Sour-Cream and Herb Sauce

Yoghurt and Fresh Herb Sauce

Yoghurt and Cucumber Sauce

Yoghurt and Scallion Sauce

Tomato Sauce

Blender Bearnaise Sauce

Mayonnaise—Blender Method

Mayonnaise—Traditional Method

Lemon Mayonnaise Sauce

Vinaigrette

Spicy Tomato Dressing

Creamy Roquefort Dressing

Brandy Butter (Hard Sauce)

This section contains sauces that go well with the salads, vegetable loafs, rissoles, etc., and desserts in this book.

With the exception of mayonnaise and Béarnaise sauce, the sauces are mostly simple and light, based on fruit and vegetable purées or mixtures of sour cream, plain yoghurt and ricotta cheese. I also find yoghurt and ricotta most useful for adding to classic mayonnaise or Béarnaise sauce to lighten them when less richness is required.

APPLE AND CRANBERRY SAUCE

If you use sweet apples for this recipe, they take the edge off the sharpness of the cranberries so you need less sugar, and the result is a pleasant, fruity sauce that's ideal with nut roasts. *Serves 6.*

1 pound sweet apples
½ cup cranberries
2–4 tablespoons sugar

Ground cinnamon—optional
Ground cloves—optional

Peel, core and slice the apples. Wash and pick over the cranberries, removing any stems. Put the apples and cranberries into a small, heavy saucepan with the sugar and cook over a gentle heat, with a lid on the saucepan, for about 10 minutes, until soft and mushy. Mash the fruits with a spoon, or purée them in a blender or food processor if you prefer a smooth sauce. Taste the mixture and add a little more sugar if necessary, and a pinch of ground cinnamon or cloves if you like the flavor.

BREAD SAUCE

1 onion, peeled	*1 tablespoon butter*
3 cloves	*1–2 tablespoons light cream*
1¼ cups milk	*Sea salt*
1 bay leaf	*Freshly ground black pepper*
2 thick slices fresh white bread,	*Grated nutmeg*
* crusts removed*	

Serves 4–6.

Put the onion, studded with the cloves, into a saucepan and add the milk and bay leaf. Bring to the boil, then take off the heat, add the slices of bread, cover and leave to one side for 15–30 minutes for the flavor to infuse. Then remove the onion and bay leaf and stir the mixture to break up the bread. Stir in the butter, cream and salt, pepper and nutmeg to taste. If you are making the sauce in advance, once you have beaten it smooth you can put back the onion and bay leaf so that they can continue to flavor the sauce until you're ready to serve it.

SPECIAL WINE SAUCE

1 tablespoon butter
1 tablespoon oil
1 small onion, peeled and chopped
1 large garlic clove, peeled and
  crushed
2 large tomatoes, preferably fresh

(unpeeled) or canned ones,
  drained
2 cups vegetable stock
⅔ cup dry red wine
Sea salt
Freshly ground black pepper

Makes 1¼ cups.
Heat the butter and oil in a medium-size saucepan and sauté the onion for 5 minutes without browning. Add the garlic and tomatoes, and cook for a further 3–4 minutes. Then pour in the stock and wine and let the mixture bubble away until the liquid has reduced by about half. Strain and season with salt and freshly ground black pepper.

MUSHROOM AND SOUR-CREAM SAUCE

This is a creamy fresh-tasting sauce that's best served warm. It is delicious with nut loaves, burgers and also with plainly cooked vegetables. *Serves 4–6.*

1 tablespoon butter
¼ pound fresh mushrooms,
  washed and chopped
1 cup sour cream

Sea salt
Freshly ground black pepper
Paprika

Melt the butter in a medium-size saucepan and sauté the mushrooms for about 5 minutes. Stir in the sour cream and salt, pepper and a little paprika to taste. Reheat gently, but don't let the sauce get too near boiling point.

SOUR-CREAM AND HERB SAUCE

This sauce is served cold, but I like it with hot dishes, such as the savory loaves, as well as with cold ones. *Makes 1¼ cups.*

⅔ cup sour cream
⅔ cup plain yoghurt
2 tablespoons chopped fresh
  herbs: parsley, chives, tarragon,

a little thyme—whatever is
  available
Sea salt
Freshly ground black pepper

Simply mix everything together and season to taste.

YOGHURT AND FRESH HERB SAUCE

This is made in exactly the same way as the preceding Sour-Cream and Herb Sauce, but you use 1¼ cups plain yoghurt and leave out the sour cream; a tablespoonful of light cream can be stirred in for added richness. I like it particularly with chopped mint or green fennel, for serving with lentil rissoles or new potatoes.

YOGHURT AND CUCUMBER SAUCE

For this variation, which is delicate and refreshing, eliminate the sour cream and use 1¼ cups plain yoghurt, 3–4 tablespoons finely chopped cucumber and 1 tablespoon chopped fresh fennel, dill, mint or whatever other fresh herb you prefer.

YOGHURT AND SCALLION SAUCE

Make as above, using, no sour cream, but 1¼ cups plain yoghurt, and 3 tablespoons chopped scallions instead of the herb mixture.

TOMATO SAUCE

I find this an extremely useful sauce to have on hand because it seems to go with so many different dishes. It's best made from fresh tomatoes, and even winter tomatoes provide good results—better than canned tomatoes. *Makes 1½ cups.*

1 tablespoon oil	Sea salt
1 onion, peeled and chopped	Freshly ground black pepper
1 clove garlic, peeled and crushed	2–3 tablespoons red wine— optional
1 pound tomatoes, peeled and chopped, or 1 can (16 ounces)	

Heat the oil in a medium-size saucepan and sauté the onion for 10 minutes, until softened but not browned. Add the garlic and tomatoes, and cook for a further 15 minutes, until the tomatoes have collapsed and reduced to a thick consistency. Sieve or purée the mixture and season with salt and pepper. This is nice sometimes with a little wine added.

BLENDER BÉARNAISE SAUCE

This is a quick version of the classic, rich, creamy sauce: first you reduce the vinegar in a saucepan to concentrate the flavor, then add it to the egg yolks in the blender or food processor and pour in the melted butter. It only takes a few minutes to make and is superb for a special occasion: I love it with the White Nut Loaf with Capers on page 124. A very pleasant variation is to stir ½ cup sour cream into the finished sauce—this lightens it, and with this addition the quantities given below will serve 8 people. *Serves 6.*

½ cup butter
2 tablespoons wine vinegar
1 tablespoon very finely chopped
  onion
8 peppercorns, lightly crushed

2 egg yolks
1 tablespoon lemon juice
Sea salt
Freshly ground black pepper

Melt the butter in a small saucepan. Heat the vinegar, onion and peppercorns together in a small saucepan until the vinegar has reduced by half. Put the egg yolks and lemon juice into the blender jar or food processor and purée until just creamy, then strain in the vinegar mixture and purée again. Now, with the blender or food processor still going, slowly pour the melted butter in. As you do so the mixture will thicken to a beautiful creamy consistency. Season with salt and pepper and serve immediately, just warm. If you need to keep this sauce warm, the safest way is to stand the saucepan in another larger saucepan or roasting pan containing very hot water.

MAYONNAISE—BLENDER METHOD

Here again, the use of a blender (or food processor) makes it easy to produce a creamy sauce every time. *Makes ¾ cup.*

1 egg
¼ teaspoon salt
¼ teaspoon dry mustard
2 or 3 grindings of black pepper
2 teaspoons wine vinegar

2 teaspoons lemon juice
¾–1 cup olive oil or a mixture
  of olive oil and soy or sunflower
  oil

Break the egg straight into the blender jar and add the salt, mustard, pepper, vinegar and lemon juice. Blend for a minute at medium speed until everything is well mixed, then turn the speed up to high and gradually add the oil, drop by drop, through the hole in the lid of the blender jar. When you've added about half the oil you will hear the sound change to a "glug-glug" noise and then you can add the rest of the oil more quickly, in a thin stream. If the consistency of the mayonnaise seems a bit too thick, you can thin it with a little more lemon juice.

MAYONNAISE—TRADITIONAL METHOD

It's more work to make mayonnaise by hand, but you do get beautiful, creamy results and it's very satisfying to see the mixture gradually thicken as you beat in the oil. *Makes ¾–1 cup.*

2–3 egg yolks
¼ teaspoon salt
¼ teaspoon dry mustard
2 or 3 grindings of black pepper
2 teaspoons wine vinegar

2 teaspoons lemon juice
¾–1 cup olive oil or a mixture of olive oil and soy or sunflower oil

Put the egg yolks into a bowl and add the salt, mustard, pepper, vinegar and lemon juice. Beat with a wire whisk for a minute or two until everything is well mixed and creamy; then start to add the oil, just a drop at a time, beating hard after each addition. When you have added about half the oil, the mixture will begin to thicken and look like mayonnaise, and then you can add the oil a little more quickly, still beating hard. Go on adding the oil until the mixture is really thick—if you use three egg yolks you will probably be able to use the full amount of oil; otherwise about ¾ cup will be enough. If the consistency of the mayonnaise seems a bit too thick, you can thin it with a little more lemon juice.

LEMON MAYONNAISE SAUCE

This sauce tastes creamy, yet is light and refreshing. You can serve it cold, with dishes like the Walnut Pâté en Croûte (page 140), or use it to coat lightly cooked vegetables before topping with crumbs and grated cheese and baking, for an extra special *au gratin* dish. *Serves 4–6.*

4 tablespoons mayonnaise
6 tablespoons sour cream
1 teaspoon prepared mustard

Juice of ½ lemon
Sea salt
Freshly ground black pepper

Just mix everything together until smooth and creamy, and season to taste.

VINAIGRETTE

When I'm making this to dress a salad, I usually make it directly in the salad bowl, mix quickly and put the salad in on top. But if you need it for pouring over a salad, or for serving with avocados, for instance, it's easiest to make it by shaking all the ingredients together in a clean screw-top jar, and for this you may want to double the quantities given here. (Any leftover dressing will keep in the fridge, but I think it's much better made fresh when you need it—and it only takes a moment.) *Serves 4.*

1 tablespoon wine vinegar—
   preferably red
3–4 tablespoons best-quality
   olive oil

Sea salt
Freshly ground black pepper

Mix everything together, adding plenty of seasoning. Some chopped fresh herbs, also a little mustard and a dash of sugar can be added to vary the flavor.

SPICY TOMATO DRESSING

This makes a very tasty dressing for kernel corn, whether served as a salad or as a side vegetable. *Makes about ½ cup.*

2 large tomatoes, skinned
2 tablespoons tomato ketchup
1 teaspoon paprika
2 tablespoons olive oil

1 tablespoon wine vinegar
Pinch of chili powder
Sea salt
Freshly ground black pepper

The easiest way to skin whole tomatoes is to drop them into boiling water for a few minutes, then let them cool. Peel the tomatoes and then just put all the ingredients into a blender or food processor and mix until smooth. Taste and check seasoning.

CREAMY ROQUEFORT DRESSING

The Roquefort gives this creamy dressing a delicious tang; it's particularly good served with ripe dessert pears. *Makes about 1 cup.*

¼ pound Roquefort cheese
⅔ cup sour cream

Sea salt
Freshly ground black pepper

Put the Roquefort cheese into a small bowl and mash with a fork. Add the sour cream and mix well, until creamy and fairly smooth. Taste and add salt and pepper if necessary: You may not need any, because the cheese is quite salty and very piquant. Stir mixture before serving.

BRANDY BUTTER (HARD SAUCE)

If you want to make a polyunsaturated version of this, use unsalted polyunsaturated margarine. To make a sauce that is less rich, you can replace half the butter (or margarine) with ricotta cheese. *Serves 6.*

½ cup unsalted butter or
   polyunsaturated margarine, soft

¼–½ cup confectioners sugar
1–2 tablespoons brandy

Beat the butter or margarine until creamy, then beat in ¼ cup of the confectioners sugar. Taste, and add a little more if you want a sweeter result. Add the brandy and beat again to make a light, fluffy cream. Put the mixture into a small serving dish and chill until needed.

Desserts

ICE CREAMS AND SHERBETS

Blueberry Sherbet with Cassis

Melon Sherbet with Crystallized Mint Leaves

Rose Sherbet

Strawberry Sherbet with Kiwi Fruit

Chestnut Ice Cream

Raspberry Ice Cream

Vanilla Ice Cream with Hot Chestnut
and Brandy Sauce

FRUIT DESSERTS

Special Fruit Salad

Fresh Mangoes

Peaches in Strawberry Purée

Pears in Cider with Ginger

Stuffed Pineapple Halves

Raspberries in Cranberry Gelatin

Kiwi Fruit in Grape Gelatin

Apricot Gelatin with Fresh Apricots
and Strawberries

Raspberry Meringue Gâteau

Strawberry Mountain

PUDDINGS, PIES AND TARTS

Gourmet Christmas Pudding

Spiced Plum Crumble

Almond-Chocolate Pie

Bakewell Tart

Black-Currant Lattice Tart with Lemon Pastry

Jeweled Fruit Tart

CAKES AND CHEESECAKES

Raspberry Victoria Sponge

Chocolate Gâteau with Hazelnuts

Candied Peel, Ginger and Almond Cake

Chocolate–Black-Currant Cheesecake

Strawberry Cheesecake

COOKIES

Crunchy Ginger Cookies

Shortbread Hearts

Ginger Thins

Vanilla Drops

This is the time when, with everyone feeling relaxed, happy and well fed, you have the opportunity to have fun and end the meal in a memorable way. That doesn't mean the dessert needs to be complicated or difficult to make; some of the most spectacular desserts are also some of the simplest to prepare: fragrant Rose Sherbet, for instance, or Peaches in Strawberry Purée.

It is also rewarding to try and think of an unusual way to flavor or garnish an ordinary dessert, making it a bit different or amusing: putting cheesecake in a chocolate crust and rippling the top with sharp-tasting fruit purée; sticking strawberries into a cone of creamy ricotta cheese to make a mountain; adding spice to a homely baked crumble topping; or serving ice cream with a hot chestnut and brandy sauce.

Ice Creams and Sherbets

BLUEBERRY SHERBET WITH CASSIS

I use fresh blueberries for this, but frozen ones are fine too. You could leave out the cassis, but it is lovely if you are serving this for a special occasion. Cassis can also be added to chilled dry white wine to make the pretty pink apéritif Kir (page 14). *Serves 6.*

1 *pound fresh blueberries and*	6 *tablespoons cassis*
½ *cup sugar*	*A little lightly whipped cream—*
2 *egg whites*	*optional*

First find a shallow, 1-quart plastic container and put this into the freezer to chill. Next prepare the blueberries. If you're using fresh ones, rinse them under cold water and take off the little stalks. Put them into a heavy saucepan with the sugar and cook them over a gentle heat for 10–15 minutes, until soft. Purée the mixture, a little at a time. Take out 3 tablespoons of this and keep to one side for the sauce. Pour the rest into the chilled container and freeze until about 1 inch around the edges is frozen; break it up with a fork. Beat the egg whites until stiff and standing in peaks but not dry; then add the frozen blueberry purée, still beating, to make a thick, fluffy mixture. Pour this back into the container and freeze again until solid.

Next make a simple sauce by mixing the reserved purée with the cassis.

Take the sherbet out of the freezer and stand it on a shelf in the fridge an hour before you want to eat it, to give it time to soften a little. Spoon into individual glasses and pour 1½ tablespoons of the sauce over each; top with a little cream if desired.

MELON SHERBET WITH CRYSTALLIZED MINT LEAVES

This is prettiest if you can find two small melons with flesh of contrasting colors—cantaloupe and honeydew, for example. Make the sherbet in two separate containers and put a spoonful of both in each bowl. Leave out the mint leaves if you haven't time to do them; but they are pretty for a special occasion and can be made in advance and stored in an airtight container. *Serves 6.*

2 small ripe melons, if possible
   one with orange flesh and one
   with green, each weighing
   about 1½ pounds

2 tablespoons fresh lemon juice
4 tablespoons sugar
2 egg whites

FOR THE MINT LEAVES:

20 fresh mint leaves
1 egg white

Sugar

Halve the melons, take out the seeds and then scoop all the flesh from the skins, keeping the two colors separate. Purée the chunks of scooped-out melon, and add half the lemon juice and half the sugar to each; taste and add a little more sugar if necessary. Spoon the two mixtures into separate containers, then freeze and finish as for the Blueberry Sherbet with Cassis (page 163), adding half the egg white to each bowl.

About 30 minutes before you want to eat the sherbet, take the containers out of the freezer and stand them on a shelf in the fridge to give them time to soften a little. Put alternate spoonfuls of each color in individual glasses and garnish with the mint leaves.

To make the mint leaves, first wash the leaves and pat dry with paper towels. Beat the egg white lightly, just to break it up. Have a saucer of sugar ready. Brush the mint leaves all over with egg white, then dip them into the sugar, coating them on both sides. Lay the leaves on a piece of waxed paper on a dry baking sheet and put them into a very cool oven 250°F, for about 2 hours to dry out, until they are crisp and brittle. Cool, then store in an airtight container until needed.

ROSE SHERBET

I wanted to make a dessert that would look like pink roses, for a summer meal, and this is the result: a delicate pink sherbet that is served in small bowls, with rose leaves around the outside resembling the calyx of the rose. Although my original idea was to make this sherbet with fragrant red rose petals from the summer garden, I have found that you can make it equally well in winter without the rose petals because most of the flavor and fragrance comes from the rose water. You will, however, need to use some other non-poisonous leaves to decorate the bowls (or omit this). *Serves 4–6.*

A handful of rose petals
2½ cups water
½ cup sugar
3–4 tablespoons rose water
A little red food coloring—
  optional

2 egg whites
A few bright green, glossy rose
  leaves

First find a shallow 1-quart plastic container and put this into the freezer to chill. Next wash the rose petals gently, then put them into a saucepan with the water. Bring up to the boil, then cover and leave for 15–30 minutes for the rose petals to infuse the water. Strain, pressing as much of the water out of the petals as you can. Measure the water and, if necessary, add enough to make 2½ cups. Put this into a saucepan with the sugar and heat gently until the sugar has dissolved. Add the rose water and a few drops of coloring to intensify the pink of the syrup if necessary—remember the mixture's color will be further toned down when the egg whites are added. Remove from the heat and leave to cool.

Pour the mixture into the chilled container and freeze until about 1 inch around the edges is frozen; break it up with a fork. Beat the egg whites until stiff and standing in peaks, but not dry; then add the frozen rose syrup, still beating, to make a thick fluffy mixture. Pour this back into the container and freeze again until solid.

Take the sherbet out of the freezer and stand it on a shelf in the fridge for 30 minutes before you want to serve it, to give it time to soften a little. Spoon the sherbet into individual glasses and tuck a few fresh green rose leaves around the edge of each, to create a rosebud effect.

STRAWBERRY SHERBET WITH KIWI FRUIT

I think this sherbet is one way of getting the best from frozen strawberries, because for this their mushiness is actually an advantage! This dessert looks particularly pretty served in a border of sliced green kiwi fruit. *Serves 6.*

1 pint fresh or 16 ounces frozen strawberries, thawed	1 tablespoon fresh lemon juice
½ cup sugar	2 egg whites
	3 kiwi fruit

Purée and strain the strawberries, adding the lemon juice to bring out the flavor and enough sugar to sweeten; then make the sherbet exactly as for the blueberry one (page 163).

About 30 minutes before you want to eat the sherbet, take it out of the freezer and stand it on a shelf in the fridge to give it time to soften a little. Peel the kiwi fruit and cut into thin slices. Spoon the sherbet into individual glasses and tuck the kiwi fruit around the edge.

CHESTNUT ICE CREAM

This is a beautiful ice cream with a delicate flavor. These quantities make a generous amount of ice cream and you could halve them if you prefer; half this would be enough for four people but I don't think it's quite enough for six. *Serves 8.*

1 can (15½ ounces) chestnut
   purée
2½ cups heavy cream

¾ cup sugar
4 tablespoons brandy

Put the chestnut purée into a bowl and beat until smooth. Then add the cream, sugar and brandy and beat everything together until thick, smooth and standing in peaks. Turn mixture into a plastic container and freeze until solid. There is no need to stir the mixture during freezing, but do take it out of the freezer and beat it 20 minutes before serving, as it is much nicer if it is not too solid.

RASPBERRY ICE CREAM

This is a favorite ice cream. It is quite rich, but I have found that you can reduce the amount of cream and use half cream and half sour cream for a lighter, healthier version. *Serves 6.*

½ pint fresh or 1 package (10
   ounces) frozen raspberries,
   thawed

½ cup sugar
1¼ cups heavy cream

Purée, then strain the raspberries to remove the seeds and make a smooth consistency. Add the sugar. Beat the cream until thick and soft peaks are formed. Fold this cream gently but thoroughly into the raspberry purée. Turn the mixture into a plastic container and put in the freezer until half frozen; then remove from the container and beat well. Return mixture to the freezing compartment and leave until completely frozen.

This ice cream is best if it's not too hard; put it on a lower shelf in the fridge for 20 minutes before you serve it.

VANILLA ICE CREAM WITH
HOT CHESTNUT AND BRANDY SAUCE

In this recipe, smooth, creamy, vanilla ice cream is topped with a hot sauce made from chestnut purée with wine and brandy. It is a wonderful dessert for special occasions. *Serves 4–6.*

2 eggs or 4 egg yolks
1¼ cups milk
⅓ cup sugar

2 teaspoons vanilla
1 cup heavy cream

FOR THE SAUCE:

½ cup unsweetened chestnut
  purée
¾ cup white wine

2 tablespoons sugar
3 tablespoons brandy

Beat the eggs in a medium-size bowl. Put the milk and sugar into a heavy saucepan and bring just up to the boil, then slowly add it to the eggs, stirring all the time. Strain the eggs and milk back into the saucepan, put back on the heat and stir for just a minute or two until the mixture thickens: this happens very quickly, so watch it and stir constantly. Leave this custard to cool.

Beat the cream until it has thickened and is standing in soft peaks, then fold this gently but thoroughly into the cooled egg custard. Pour the mixture into a plastic container and freeze until it's setting well around the edges. Then scrape the ice cream into a bowl and beat it thoroughly. Put the ice cream back into the container and freeze until it's firm. Take the ice cream out of the fridge at the beginning of the meal and beat it before serving as it is much nicer if it is not too solid.

To make the sauce, put the chestnut purée into a saucepan and break it up with a fork; then gradually stir in the wine and sugar. Set the pan over a gentle heat and stir until you have a thick, creamy consistency: this can all be done well in advance. Just before you want to serve the ice cream, reheat the chestnut mixture, beating it smooth, and add the brandy.

Fruit Desserts

SPECIAL FRUIT SALAD

I think a fresh fruit salad, made with interesting fruits that contrast
with and complement each other in color and flavor, is most delicious.
The exact composition depends, of course, on what is available, but I
like to include strawberries, black grapes or cherries when possible,
and also kiwi fruit because its vivid green provides such a pretty color
contrast. The apricot liqueur gives a lovely flavor and draws out the
juices from the fruits, but the dessert is also good made with one of the
orange liqueurs, such as Cointreau; if you don't want to use liqueur
you can use sweet white wine or orange juice. *Serves 6–8.*

4 kiwi fruit	*1 medium-size ripe pineapple*
½ pint fresh strawberries	*1¼ cups apricot nectar*
2 medium-size ripe mangoes	*6–8 tablespoons apricot liqueur*

Peel the kiwi fruit and cut the flesh into thin rounds; wash and hull
the strawberries, halving or quartering any large ones; cut the mangoes
in half and remove the pits; peel the flesh and dice; peel and dice the
pineapple, cutting away any hard central core. Put all the fruit into a

serving dish and add the apricot nectar and liqueur. Chill the fruit salad until ready to serve—it's best if you can let it stand for a couple of hours so that the juices can be drawn out and the flavors can blend.

FRESH MANGOES

If you can find some really ripe medium-size mangoes, they make a lovely dessert that always seems to please people. The mangoes should feel really soft to the touch; like avocadoes, they will ripen in a cupboard if put into a paper bag and left for two or three days.

1 medium-large mango serves
  2 people

Don't prepare the mangoes until just before the meal. Then slice each mango down from the top, cutting about ¼ inch each side of the stem. The object of this is to make the cuts each side of the large flat pit in the center. Ease the two halves apart and place each on a dish. You eat the mango as you would an avocado, by scooping the flesh out with a small spoon, and it's delicious.

PEACHES IN STRAWBERRY PUREE

This dish consists of juicy, ripe peach slices bathed in a pink strawberry purée. It's another dessert that's very simple to make and a perfect way to use frozen strawberries. It's also delicious made with ripe pears instead of peaches. *Serves 6.*

6 large, ripe peaches   *¼ cup sugar*
2 tablespoons lemon juice
1 pint fresh or 16 ounces frozen
  strawberries

Cover the peaches with boiling water; leave for 2 minutes, then drain. Slip the skins off using a sharp knife. Halves the peaches and remove the pits, then slice the flesh. Put the slices into a pretty glass bowl or six individual ones and sprinkle with half the lemon juice to preserve the color.

Wash and hull the strawberries, then put them into a blender or food processor with the rest of the lemon juice and reduce to a purée. Press the mixture through a strainer, to make it really smooth, then add the sugar gradually—taste the mixture, as you may not need it all. Pour the strawberry purée over the peaches.

PEARS IN CIDER WITH GINGER

The best pears for this are pears that are firm but sweet. If you don't like ginger you can leave it out. *Serves 6.*

6 firm, sweet pears   ¼ cup crystallized ginger
3¾ cups apple cider

Peel the pears, leaving them whole and with their stems still attached. Put them into a large, heavy saucepan and pour in the cider—it should cover them. Bring them up to the boil, then turn the heat down and leave them to simmer, without a lid on the saucepan, for about 30 minutes, until the pears feel tender when pierced with a sharp knife and there is just a little syrupy-looking cider left. Add the ginger and let stand until cold. Serve chilled, with a bowl of lightly whipped cream.

STUFFED PINEAPPLE HALVES

One small pineapple is enough to serve two people. Cut in half, right through the center, including the leafy green top. Cut and scoop out the flesh, and mix with black grapes or ripe strawberries. The stuffed pineapples look very pretty arranged like the spokes of a wheel on a large round plate. *Serves 6.*

3 *small pineapples with attractive*   1 ½ *cups small, ripe strawberries*
   leafy tops   *or black grapes*

Wash and dry the pineapples, then slice each in half right through the green top. Using a sharp knife and a spoon, scoop out the flesh and cut into small pieces, discarding any hard core. Wash the strawberries or grapes. Halve and pit the grapes; hull the strawberries and cut them as necessary. Mix the pineapple pieces with the strawberries or grapes and pile the mixture back into the pineapple shells. Arrange the stuffed pineapples on a large, flat plate.

RASPBERRIES IN CRANBERRY GELATIN

This is a refreshing dessert: raspberries set in a gelatin made from cranberry juice. If you are using frozen raspberries that haven't thawed, the gelatin will set almost immediately, making this a good emergency dish! *Serves 6–8.*

2 *cups fresh* or *frozen raspberries*   2 *teaspoons agar agar*
3 *cups cranberry juice*   *Whipped cream*
2–4 *tablespoons sugar*   *Pistachio nuts*

Divide the raspberries among six or eight small dishes. Put the juice into a large saucepan, with enough sugar to sweeten, and bring to the boil; then sprinkle the agar agar (to make the gelatin set quickly) over the top, a little at a time, stirring after each addition to help the powder dissolve. (The mixture will tend to froth up, which is why you need a fairly large saucepan.) When all the agar agar has been added, let the mixture boil for 1 minute, then remove from the heat and strain over the raspberries. Leave to cool, then chill. Top the gelatin with whipped cream and a few green pistachio nuts, shelled and chopped, to show their pretty green color.

KIWI FRUIT IN GRAPE GELATIN

Kiwi fruit is so pretty and this dish makes the most of its flowerlike appearance. *Serves 6–8.*

4 kiwi fruit	*2 level teaspoons agar agar*
3 cups white grape juice	*Whipped cream*
2 tablespoons sugar	*Pistachio nuts*

Make the gelatin exactly as for the preceding recipe, arranging the slices of kiwi fruit attractively in the bowls.

APRICOT GELATIN WITH FRESH APRICOTS AND STRAWBERRIES

For this gelatin you need apricot nectar, available in large supermarkets and delicatessens. *Serves 6–8.*

8 ripe apricots	*2 teaspoons agar agar*
3 cups apricot nectar	*Whipped cream*
2 tablespoons sugar	*6–8 ripe strawberries, for garnish*

Peel the apricots by plunging them into boiling water for 2 minutes, then draining and slipping off the skins with a sharp knife. Halve the apricots, remove the pits, then slice the flesh. Make the gelatin exactly as for Raspberries in Cranberry Gelatin (page 173). Put the apricots into individual bowls, pour the apricot nectar over and leave to set. Garnish with a swirl of whipped cream and some ripe strawberries.

RASPBERRY MERINGUE GÂTEAU

This is a superbly rich and indulgent dessert that nobody ought to eat
but everyone loves for a special occasion. It's also delicious made with
sweet ripe blackberries, either freshly picked or frozen. *Serves 6.*

3 *egg whites*	2 *cups fresh or frozen raspberries,*
¾ *cup sugar*	*thawed*
1½ *cups heavy cream*	*Confectioners sugar*

First make the meringue. Beat the egg whites until peaks form, then
beat in half the sugar until the whites are stiff, making a smooth,
glossy mixture. Fold in the rest of the sugar. Draw two circles, 8 inches
in diameter, on waxed paper. Spoon the meringue to cover the circles
in an even layer. Bake in a very cool oven, 250°F, for 2–3 hours,
until crisp and dry but not brown. Let the meringue circles cool completely, then peel off the paper. Store in an airtight container until
needed for filling.

To fill the meringue, put one of the layers on a flat serving dish.
Whip the cream until it is standing in firm peaks. Spread half this
mixture over the meringue and top with half the raspberries. Cover
with the other meringue circle and the rest of the cream and raspberries, and dust the top with confectioners sugar. Serve as soon as
possible.

STRAWBERRY MOUNTAIN

When strawberries are in season this makes an impressive dessert. You
can make the ricotta cheese base in advance, but it's best not to add the
strawberries more than an hour before you want to serve the dessert.
You must use heavy cream because the mixture needs to be firm. Need-
less to say, this is a very rich dish. *Serves 6.*

1½ cups ricotta cheese
1½ cups heavy cream
2 tablespoons sugar
1 teaspoon vanilla

1 pint small ripe strawberries,
 washed and hulled
Confectioners sugar

Put the ricotta cheese into a bowl. Add the heavy cream, sugar and vanilla and beat together until light and thick enough to hold its shape well. Pile the mixture up into a cone shape on a flat serving dish. Chill until required. Just before you want to serve the dessert, stud the cone all over with the strawberries so that it is completely covered, and sift a little confectioners sugar over the top.

Puddings, Pies and Tarts

GOURMET CHRISTMAS PUDDING

This recipe is an adaptation of Escoffier's Christmas pudding, which I like because it is light both in flavor and texture. *Serves 8.*

4 cups soft whole-wheat bread
   crumbs
½ cup polyunsaturated margarine
1 cup whole-wheat flour
½ teaspoon baking powder
2 teaspoons pumpkin pie spice
4 tablespoons sugar
1 medium-size cooking apple,
   peeled and chopped
1 cup sultanas, or golden raisins
1 cup raisins
1 cup currants

½ cup chopped candied peel
¼ cup chopped crystallized
   ginger
Grated rind of ½ small orange
Grated rind of ½ small lemon
¼ cup slivered almonds
1 egg
1 tablespoon orange juice
1 tablespoon lemon juice
4 tablespoons brandy
1 cup beer

Put the bread crumbs, margarine, flour, baking powder, spice, sugar, apple, dried fruit, grated rinds and nuts into a large bowl and mix well. Beat the egg with the orange and lemon juice, brandy and beer, until well blended. Add the dry ingredients and mix well, then cover and leave for several hours or overnight.

Next day mix again and spoon into a greased 1½-quart bowl or steamed-pudding mold (these come with fitted lids and are available in kitchen specialty shops). If you're using a bowl, cover with greased waxed paper and foil and secure well with tied string. Steam for 4 hours.

Store in a cool, dry place; steam for another 3 hours before serving.

SPICED PLUM CRUMBLE

This is just a spicy version of an old favorite that always seems to be popular. *Serves 6.*

1½ *pounds plums*   ⅓ *cup sugar*

FOR THE TOPPING:

2 *cups whole-wheat flour*   ⅓ *cup sugar*
1 *teaspoon baking powder*   6 *tablespoons polyunsaturated*
1 *teaspoon ground allspice*   *margarine*

Preheat the oven to 375°F. Halve the plums and take out the pits. Put the plums into a shallow baking dish and sprinkle with the sugar.

To make the topping, sift the flour, baking powder and allspice into a bowl, adding the bran left in the sieve too. Mix in the sugar and then cut in the margarine—it may be easiest to use a fork for this— until the mixture looks like fine bread crumbs. Sprinkle this crumb mixture over the top of the plums in an even layer and press down lightly. Bake for 45 minutes.

ALMOND-CHOCOLATE PIE

This is an indulgence for chocolate-lovers like me: a rich chocolate cream in a crisp crust of light almond shortbread. *Serves 6–8.*

FOR THE CRUST:

½ cup whole-wheat flour
½ cup ground almonds
3 tablespoons sugar

6 tablespoons butter or
    polyunsaturated margarine

FOR THE FILLING:

6 squares (6 ounces) semisweet
   chocolate

1 cup heavy cream

First make the crust. Preheat the oven to 350°F. Butter an 8-inch pie plate. Put the flour, almonds and sugar into a bowl and gradually work in the butter or margarine to make a dough. Roll out to fit the pie plate; press gently into the pie plate, trim the edges and prick the bottom. Bake for 25–30 minutes, until golden brown and crisp. Cool.

To make the filling, break the chocolate into a bowl (or the top of a double boiler), set the bowl over a saucepan of gently simmering water and leave until the chocolate has melted. Cool slightly, but do not allow to harden. Put the cream into another bowl, pour in the chocolate and beat them together until you have a light, fluffy mixture. Pour this into the cooled crust. Chill until the chocolate mixture has set.

BAKEWELL TART

This traditional tart, with its crisp pastry covered with jam and a light almond sponge, makes a very satisfactory dessert either hot or cold. *Serves 6.*

FOR THE PASTRY:

1½ cups whole-wheat flour
6 tablespoons polyunsaturated
   margarine or butter

1½ tablespoons cold water

FOR THE FILLING:

3 tablespoons raspberry jam
½ cup margarine
½ cup sugar
2 eggs

¼ cup unbleached all-purpose
   flour
½ cup ground almonds
A few almonds slivered

To make the pastry, sift the flour into a large bowl, and just tip in the bran left in the sieve. Blend the margarine or butter into the flour, using a pastry blender or a fork, until the mixture resembles fine bread crumbs. Add the cold water and press the mixture together to form a dough. If there's time, refrigerate for 30 minutes (this makes it easier to roll out but isn't essential).

Preheat the oven to 425°F, and, if possible, place a heavy baking sheet on the top shelf to heat up with the oven. Roll out the pastry and ease it into an 8-inch lightly greased quiche/tart pan; trim edges. Spread pastry bottom with the jam. Put the margarine, sugar, eggs, flour and ground almonds into a bowl and beat for 2 minutes, until light and creamy. Spoon this mixture over the jam and sprinkle with slivered almonds.

Bake in the preheated oven for 5 minutes, then turn the oven down to 350°F, and bake for a further 30–35 minutes, until golden and firm to the touch. Serve hot or cold, with light cream if liked.

BLACK-CURRANT LATTICE TART WITH LEMON PASTRY

Use a good quality black-currant jam or one of the lovely no-added-sugar jams from health-food shops instead of the fruit, if you prefer: the tart is sweeter if you use jam. *Serves 6.*

1½ cups whole-wheat flour
Finely grated rind of 1 lemon

6 tablespoons polyunsaturated
   margarine or butter
1½ tablespoons cold water

FOR THE FILLING:

1 13½-ounce (or thereabouts) jar
   black-currant jam

Milk and sugar, for glaze

First make the pastry: sift the flour into a large bowl, and just tip in the bran left in the sieve. Add the lemon rind, then blend the margarine or butter into the flour using a pastry blender or a fork until the mixture resembles fine bread crumbs. Add the cold water and press the mixture together to form a dough. If there's time, refrigerate for 30 minutes (this makes it easier to roll out but isn't essential).

Preheat the oven to 425°F, and, if possible, place a heavy baking sheet on the top rack to heat up with the oven. Roll out the pastry and ease it into an 8-inch lightly greased pie pan; trim edges.

Spread the black-currant jam evenly in the shell. Gather up and reroll the pastry trimmings, cut into thin strips, and arrange in a lattice on top. Brush the strips with milk and sprinkle with a little sugar.

Bake in the preheated oven for 5 minutes, then turn the oven down to 350°F, and bake for a further 30–35 minutes, until the pastry is golden brown. Serve hot or cold, with light cream if liked.

JEWELED FRUIT TART

Serves 6–8.

FOR THE CRUST:

¾ cup whole-wheat flour
¾ cup ground almonds
3 tablespoons sugar

½ cup butter or polyunsaturated
   margarine

1 cup small, ripe strawberries, washed and hulled	6 tablespoons red-currant or raspberry jelly
1 cup raspberries	

First make the crust. Preheat the oven to 350°F. Butter an 8-inch tart/quiche pan. Put the flour, almonds and sugar into a bowl and gradually work in the butter or margarine to make a dough. Roll out fairly thickly to fit the tart pan; press gently into the pan, trim the edges and prick the bottom. Bake the crust for 25–30 minutes, until golden brown and crisp. Cool.

To finish the tart, arrange the strawberries and red currants in concentric circles on top of the pastry, ending with a strawberry in the center. Melt the red currant jelly in a small, heavy saucepan over a gentle heat, then brush evenly over the top of the fruit to glaze. Let stand until the glaze has set.

Cakes and Cheesecakes

These desserts have been chosen as the ideal finishing touch to the feasts you will be putting together with the earlier recipes in this volume.

RASPBERRY VICTORIA SPONGE

A light layer cake filled with fresh or frozen raspberries and whipped cream and sprinkled with confectioners sugar, this is lovely for a special summer party. If you want to cut down on calories, you can replace the cream with ricotta cheese, beaten with a little milk until light and creamy; or use half cream and half sour cream. *Makes two 8-inch layers.*

1¾ cup whole-wheat flour
2½ teaspoons baking powder
2 eggs
1 cup sugar

½ cup polyunsaturated
   margarine
¾ cup milk

1 cup heavy cream, whipped   *Confectioners sugar*
1 pint fresh or 10 ounces frozen
    raspberries, thawed, and
    drained if frozen

Preheat the oven to 350°F. Line two 8-inch cake pans with waxed paper and brush with oil. Sift the flour and baking powder into a bowl, then put in all the remaining cake ingredients and beat by hand or using an electric mixer for 2–3 minutes, until light and creamy.

Divide the mixture between the two pans and smooth the tops. Bake for 20 minutes, until the cakes are well risen and spring back when pressed lightly in the center. Turn the cakes out onto a wire rack to cool, then strip off the paper. Spread one of the cakes with half the cream and arrange the raspberries on top; sprinkle with a little of the confectioners sugar, then spread with the rest of the cream and place the other cake on top. Sprinkle with more confectioners sugar. Serve as soon as possible.

CHOCOLATE GÂTEAU
WITH HAZELNUTS

This is a luscious cake—rich and very fattening, but wonderful for a special occasion. *Makes two 8-inch layers.*

1½ cups whole-wheat flour   *1 cup sugar*
4 tablespoons cocoa powder   *¾ cup polyunsaturated*
2 teaspoons baking powder   *margarine*
1 teaspoon baking soda   *1 cup milk*
3 eggs

1 egg
⅔ cup milk
⅓ cup sugar
4 squares (4 ounces) semisweet
  chocolate
1 cup unsalted butter or unsalted
  polyunsaturated margarine,
  softened

½ cup chopped roasted hazelnuts
  (see page 22)
A few whole hazelnuts,
  preferably roasted and with
  the skins rubbed off

Preheat the oven to 350°F. Line two 8-inch cake pans with waxed paper and brush with oil. Sift the flour, cocoa, baking powder and baking soda into a bowl, then put in all the remaining cake ingredients and beat by hand or electric mixer for 2–3 minutes, until light and creamy. Divide the mixture between the pans and smooth the tops. Bake for 30 minutes, until the cakes are well risen and spring back when pressed lightly in the center. Turn the cakes out onto a wire rack to cool, then strip off the paper.

Meanwhile make the butter cream for the filling and topping. Put the egg, milk and sugar into a small saucepan and beat together until smooth. Heat gently, stirring all the time, until just beginning to thicken. Remove from the heat. Break up the chocolate and add this to the custard mixture: the heat of the custard will melt it. Stir occasionally, then leave to one side until cool. Beat the butter or margarine until light and fluffy, then gradually beat in the cold chocolate custard mixture.

Put 3 rounded tablespoons of the butter cream into a pastry bag fitted with a large star tip; leave to one side for the moment. Split each of the cakes in half, so that you have four layers. Sandwich the cakes together with some of the butter cream. Spread the sides of the cake with butter cream and coat with nuts. Cover the top of the cake with the remaining cream. Pipe the reserved butter cream in the center and around the top edge of the cake. Decorate with a few whole hazelnuts.

CANDIED PEEL, GINGER AND ALMOND CAKE

This cake is rather an indulgence on my part because I have included three of my favorite cake ingredients: candied peel, almonds and crystallized ginger! It makes a pleasant change from the usual Dundee cake. *Makes one 8-inch layer.*

2 cups whole-wheat flour
1 teaspoon baking powder
¾ cup polyunsaturated margarine
1 cup soft brown sugar
3 eggs, beaten
1 cup chopped mixed candied peel
1 cup roughly chopped
  crystallized ginger

Grated rind of 1 lemon
1 cup ground almonds
½ cup slivered almonds
½ cup milk
Honey, for glaze

Preheat the oven to 350°F. Line a deep 8-inch round cake pan with greased waxed paper. Sift the flour with the baking powder and mix in the bran left in the sieve. Cream the margarine and sugar until light and fluffy, then slowly add the beaten eggs, one at a time, beating constantly and adding a little flour if the mixture starts to separate. Fold in the flour and all the other ingredients. Spoon the mixture into the prepared pan and bake for 2 hours, until a warmed skewer inserted into the center of the cake comes out clean. Cool for 5 minutes in the pan, then turn out onto a wire rack to finish cooling. Peel off the paper when the cake is cold, then warm a little honey and brush all over the cake to make it look shiny and appetizing.

CHOCOLATE–BLACK-CURRANT CHEESECAKE

This is a delicious cheesecake: a smooth creamy cheese mixture swirled with black-currant jam on a crisp crust of chocolate and nuts. It's easy to make and needs no cooking. *Serves 6.*

FOR THE CRUST:

1 cup crushed vanilla wafers

4 squares (4 ounces) semisweet
   baking chocolate, melted

½ cup chopped mixed nuts

FOR THE FILLING:

1½ cups ricotta cheese

1 cup heavy cream

3 tablespoons black-currant or
   blueberry jam

A little grated chocolate

To make the crust, put all the ingredients into a bowl and mix together, then spread over the bottom of an 8-inch springform pan. Refrigerate while you make the filling.

To make the filling, stir the ricotta cheese and cream together. Lightly mix in the black-currant jam, just swirling it. Don't mix it in too much. Pour the filling into the crust. Chill for at least 2 hours, preferably overnight. Remove the sides of the tin; sprinkle with grated chocolate to serve.

STRAWBERRY CHEESECAKE

This recipe makes a big, luscious cheesecake with a shiny strawberry topping—a wonderful dessert for a summer party. *Serves 8–10.*

FOR THE CRUST:

1½ cups crushed vanilla wafers

6 tablespoons butter or

polyunsaturated margarine,
melted

FOR THE FILLING:

2 cups ricotta cheese

3 eggs

1 teaspoon vanilla

½ cup sugar

⅔ cup sour cream

1 cup sour cream
1 pint fresh strawberries,
  washed and hulled

6–8 tablespoons red-currant
jelly

Preheat the oven to 300°F. Combine the crushed wafers with the butter or margarine. Press the wafer mixture evenly over the bottom of an 8-inch spring form pan. Refrigerate while you make the filling.

To make the filling, purée everything in your blender or food processor for a minute, until smooth. Alternatively, put the cheese into a large bowl, then add the eggs, vanilla, sugar and sour cream and beat thoroughly to a smooth consistency. Pour the mixture into the pan on top of the crushed wafers.

Bake the cheesecake in the bottom third of the oven for 1½ hours, until it looks set and feels firm to a very light touch. Cool, then spread the sour cream for topping over the cheesecake. Chill for 2–3 hours.

To finish the cheesecake, arrange the strawberries evenly over the top. Melt the red-currant jelly in a small, heavy saucepan over a gentle heat, then brush over the strawberries in a thin layer to glaze. Refrigerate. To serve, carefully remove the cheesecake from the pan.

Cookies

CRUNCHY GINGER COOKIES

Crunchy ginger cookies are delightful served with creamy desserts, for children's parties or picnics. These are generally popular and are quick and easy to make. If you find the texture of whole-wheat flour rather heavy, don't put back the bran after you have sifted the flour, but use it to "flour" the baking sheet. That way you will still be getting the balanced goodness of the whole flour, but with a lighter texture. *Makes about 30.*

1 cup whole-wheat flour	*1 cup rolled oats*
1 teaspoon baking powder	*½ cup polyunsaturated margarine*
1 teaspoon ground ginger	*1 cup brown sugar*
½ teaspoon baking soda	*1 rounded tablespoon honey*

Preheat the oven to 350°F. Sift the flour, baking powder, ginger and baking soda into a bowl, keeping the residue of bran from the sieve to one side for the moment; add the oats to the mixture. Put the margarine, sugar and honey in a medium-size heavy saucepan and heat gently until the margarine melts. Remove from the heat and stir in the flour mixture. Grease a baking sheet with butter and sprinkle with the reserved bran from the sieve. Form teaspoons of the mixture into small balls, place well apart on the prepared baking sheet and flatten each with a fork. Bake for 15 minutes. Leave to cool on the tray for 5 minutes, then transfer to a wire rack to finish cooling.

SHORTBREAD HEARTS

These are nice crisp cookies that melt in your mouth and are good with creamy desserts. Of course you don't have to make these heart-shaped; they are also good frosted, for children's parties in which case you'll probably be cutting them out in the shapes of teddy bears, engines, cars and so on! *Makes about 60 small hearts.*

1½ cups whole-wheat flour
¼ cup sugar

10 tablespoons butter or polyunsaturated margarine

Preheat the oven to 350°F. Sift the flour into a bowl, keeping the residue of bran from the sieve to one side for the moment. Add the sugar, then blend in the butter or margarine with a fork until the mixture looks like fine bread crumbs. Press mixture gently together to make a dough. Sprinkle a board with the bran from the sieve, turn the dough onto this and knead lightly; then roll out to a thickness of about ⅛ inch and stamp into hearts (or other shapes) with a cookie cutter. Put the shapes on a baking sheet and bake for 15–20 minutes. Leave to cool on the baking sheet for 5 minutes, then transfer to a wire rack to finish cooling.

GINGER THINS

This is really a variation of the Shortbread Hearts and made in exactly the same way except that you sift 1 teaspoonful of ground ginger with the flour and increase the amount of sugar to ⅓ cup.

VANILLA DROPS

These are melt-in-the-mouth cookies that are piped onto a baking sheet.
Makes 12.

¾ cup whole-wheat flour
¼ cup all-purpose unbleached
  flour
½ cup sugar

6 tablespoons polyunsaturated
  margarine
1 teaspoon vanilla
Confectioners sugar

Preheat the oven to 350°F. Sift the flours into a bowl, then add all the remaining ingredients and beat together to make a soft, light mixture. Spoon this mixture into a pastry bag fitted with a large star tip, and pipe stars onto a lightly greased baking sheet. Bake for about 20 minutes, until set and golden brown. Leave to cool on the baking sheet for 5 minutes, then transfer to a wire rack to finish cooling.

Breads

Herb Bread
Soft Bread Rolls
Freezer Rolls
Melba Toast
Cheese, Mustard and Sesame Scones
Baby Scones
Whole-Wheat Cheese Straws

Perhaps more down-to-earth, but still delicious, homemade breads make a real contribution to any meal. The various rolls and the Cheese, Mustard and Sesame Scones, can all be made fairly quickly. The fragrant Herb Bread, though more time-consuming to make, fills the kitchen with a wonderful fragrance of herbs as it bakes. This is delicious served warm with soups and cheese dishes. Don't forget, too, that most breads and rolls can be baked, frozen, and then heated through when you're ready to serve them, without sacrificing their texture and taste.

HERB BREAD

Served warm from the oven, this bread is delicious with soup, especially the Cauliflower Soup with Almonds or the Jerusalem Artichoke Soup. This bread takes just 2 hours to make from start to finish. *Makes one loaf.*

6 tablespoons milk
6 tablespoons hot water
1 package active dry yeast
½ teaspoon sugar
2½ cups whole-wheat flour
4 teaspoons sugar
1 teaspoon salt
2 tablespoons butter or

polyunsaturated margarine,
melted and cooled to room
temperature.
1 small onion, peeled and finely
grated
½ teaspoon dried oregano
½ teaspoon dried savory

Put the milk and water into a bowl, then sprinkle in the yeast and sugar; stir once. Leave to one side for 10 minutes, until the yeast has frothed up with a head, like a glass of beer.

Put the flour, sugar and salt into a large bowl. Make a well in the center and pour in the yeast mixture. Add the melted butter, onion and herbs. Stir with a wooden spoon to form a soft dough that leaves the sides of the bowl clean. Turn the dough out onto a floured working surface and knead for 10 minutes, until the texture becomes smooth and pliable. Place the dough in a greased bowl and turn to coat. Cover with plastic wrap and set aside in a warm draft-free place to rise, until doubled in size (about 45 minutes).

Preheat the oven to 450°F. Take the dough out of the bowl and press it firmly all over with your knuckles to "knock back" the dough and remove any large pockets of air. Knead for 2 minutes, then form the dough into a rectangle, roll it over so that the seam is underneath and drop it into a greased 8 x 4-inch loaf pan, pressing the corners down well into the pan so that the center is nice and rounded. Cover with a damp cloth or a piece of plastic wrap and leave in a warm place for 20–30 minutes to rise. Bake in the preheated oven for 10 minutes, then turn the oven setting down to 400°F, and bake the bread for a further 25 minutes. Turn the loaf out onto a wire rack to cool. It's nicest served warm from the oven, cut into thick slices.

SOFT BREAD ROLLS

These whole-wheat rolls turn out light and fluffy and are easy to make. If you like them, you can make very good hot cross buns from this recipe by adding a teaspoonful of mixed spice and ½ cup dried fruit, then brushing the buns when they come out of the oven with a glaze made by melting 2 tablespoons of sugar in 1 tablespoon of milk. *Makes 12 rolls.*

1 *package active dry yeast*	2 *tablespoons butter or vegetable*
1 *teaspoon sugar*	*margarine, melted and cooled*
⅔ *cup lukewarm milk*	*to room temperature*
3 *cups whole-wheat flour*	1 *egg, beaten*
1 *teaspoon salt*	

Put the milk into a bowl, then stir in the sugar and sprinkle in the yeast; stir once. Leave to one side for 10 minutes, until the yeast has frothed up with a head, like a glass of beer.

Put the flour and salt into a large bowl. Make a well in the center and pour in the yeast mixture, the melted butter and beaten egg. Mix together to form a soft dough. Turn the dough out onto a floured working surface and knead for 10 minutes, until the texture becomes smooth and pliable. Place the dough in a greased bowl and turn to coat. Cover the bowl with a piece of plastic wrap and leave to rise at room temperature for 1½ hours.

Preheat the oven to 425°F. Take the dough out of the bowl and press it firmly all over with your knuckles to "knock back" and remove any large pockets of air. Knead for 2 minutes, then divide the dough into 24 pieces and form each into a smooth roll. Place the rolls about 1 inch apart on a greased baking sheet, cover with plastic wrap or a clean cloth and leave in a warm place to rise for 30 minutes. Bake for 20 minutes, until the rolls are browned and sound hollow when you turn one over and tap it on the base.

FREEZER ROLLS

It's very convenient to be able to take a batch of partly cooked rolls from the freezer, finish them off in the oven and serve them fresh and warm. You can do this if you bake them first at a low temperature, then freeze them and finish them off as usual when you need them. Follow the previous recipe but bake the rolls at 300°F for 20 minutes, just to "set" the rolls. Cool them completely, then pack in plastic bags and freeze. To use, let the rolls thaw out at room temperature for 45–60 minutes, then bake at 450°F, for 10 minutes. They can be cooked while still frozen, if you're desperate, but may take a bit longer, about 15 minutes.

MELBA TOAST

You can make excellent melba toast from sliced whole-wheat bread and it makes a lovely crunchy accompaniment to creamy dips and pâtés. It's delicious, and people always eat more than you think they will, so make plenty!

1 or 2 slices whole-wheat bread
  for each person

Preheat the oven to 400°F. Toast the bread on one side in the usual way, then lay the piece of toast flat on a board and, using a sharp knife and a sawing motion, cut the bread in half horizontally. Place the toast halves, uncooked side uppermost, on a baking sheet and bake for 7–10 minutes, until they are crisp and brown all over, curling up at the edges. Cool.

CHEESE, MUSTARD AND SESAME SCONES

These scones can be made from start to finish in 20–30 minutes, and they are lovely for serving with soup to make it a hearty meal, or with a vegetable gratin or stew. They are also nice to take on a picnic. *Makes about 12.*

2 cups whole-wheat flour
4 teaspoons baking powder
1 teaspoon dry mustard
½ teaspoon sea salt

¼ cup polyunsaturated margarine
1¼ cups grated Cheddar cheese
½–⅔ cup buttermilk
Sesame seeds

Preheat the oven to 425°F. Sift the flour, baking powder, mustard and salt into a large bowl, adding the bran left in the sieve, too. Using a pastry blender or fork, cut the margarine into the flour until the mixture looks like fine bread crumbs. Lightly mix in 1 cup of the grated cheese, then enough of the buttermilk to make a soft dough that leaves the sides of the bowl clean. Sprinkle a board with sesame seeds and turn the dough out onto them. Knead the dough briefly, then roll it out in the sesame seeds to a thickness of about 1 inch, pressing the sesame seeds into the dough and turning the dough over so that both sides are coated. Use a 2-inch cutter to cut the dough into rounds. Place the rounds on a floured baking sheet and sprinkle the rest of the cheese on top of the scones. Bake in the top third of the oven for about 12 minutes, until the scones have risen and are golden brown. Cool on a wire rack.

BABY SCONES

These scones can be made from the same mixture as in the preceding recipe, but cut out with a tiny round cutter measuring ½ inch in diameter; or you can leave out the cheese and add ¼ cup sugar instead, for a sweet version. They are a bit fiddly to make but are very suitable for a buffet or cocktail party, split and topped with various sweet and savory dips. Using a small cutter, the quantities above should yield about thirty scones, and they will take about 10 minutes to bake.

WHOLE-WHEAT CHEESE STRAWS

Cheese straws are always popular and ideal for serving with drinks and dips. *Makes about 80.*

1 cup whole-wheat flour
½ teaspoon baking powder
A good pinch of cayenne
Sea salt
Freshly ground black pepper

6 tablespoons butter or
   polyunsaturated margarine
¾ cup finely grated Cheddar
   cheese

Preheat the oven to 400°F. Sift the flour with the baking powder, cayenne, salt and freshly ground black pepper, adding the bran left in the sieve, too. Using a pastry blender or fork, cut the butter or margarine into the flour until the mixture looks like fine bread crumbs. Lightly mix in the grated cheese and press mixture together to make a soft but firm dough. Turn the dough out onto a lightly floured board; knead briefly and then roll out about ⅛ inch thick and cut into straws about ⅛ inch wide and 2 inches long. Put the straws on a floured baking sheet and bake in the preheated oven for about 7–10 minutes, until they are crisp and golden brown. Cool on a wire rack—they will get crisper as they cool.

Index

banana, peanut and scallion salad,
   68–69
barbecues, 10–12
beans:
   dried, nutritional value of, 22
   kidney, in salad with carrots and
      walnuts, 76–77
   navy, in salad with herbs, 74
   and ripe-olive pâté with hard-boiled
      eggs, 47–48
   see also lentils; lima beans
Béarnaise sauce, 153–54
beets:
   in salad with apples, celery and
      creamy topping with walnuts, 69
   spiced, with apples and cranberries,
      83–84
black currants:
   and chocolate cheesecake, 186–87
   lattice tart with lemon pastry, 180–81
blueberry sherbet with cassis, 163–64
braised cucumber with walnuts, 89–90
brandy butter, 158
breads, 192–200
   baby scones, 199
   cheese, mustard and sesame scones,
      198–99
   freezer rolls, 197–98
   herb, 195–96
   melba toast, 198
   sauce, 150
   sesame toast, 48–49
   soft rolls, 196–97
   whole-wheat cheese straws, 200
Brussels sprouts, 84–86
   with chestnuts and wine sauce, 84–85
   festive, 85
   purée of, 86
buffets, 12–13
burgers, lentil and mushroom, 108–9
butter:
   brandy, 158
   nutritional value of, 22

cabbage, 86–88
   buttered, with garlic and coriander,
      86–87
   Chinese, with scallions, 72, 87
   red, with apples baked in cider, 88
   salad with nuts and raisins, 71

cakes, 183–85
   candied peel, ginger and almond, 186
   chocolate gâteau with hazelnuts,
      184–85
   raspberry meringue gâteau, 175
   raspberry Victoria sponge, 183–84
   see also cheesecakes
capers, white nut loaf with, 124–25
carrots:
   in deep-dish vegetable pie, 136–37
   oven-baked, 88–89
   root vegetables with turmeric and
      coconut sauce, 97–98
   in salad with apples and mint, 70–71
   in salad with kidney beans and
      walnuts, 76–77
   in soup with apples and chervil,
      31–32
   in spiced vegetables with dhal sauce,
      116–17
cashew balls with avocados and cottage
   cheese in tomato dressing, 42–43
cassis, 14–15, 163–64
cauliflower:
   in quiche with Stilton and walnuts,
      133–34
   soup, with almonds, 32
celeriac and potato purée, 96
celery:
   in salad with beets, apples and creamy
      topping with walnuts, 69
   soup, 33
cheese, 17, 21–22
   cheddar, in dip with red wine, 49
   Cheddar filling, colored pinwheels
      with, 61–62
   cottage, with avocados and cashew
      balls in tomato dressing, 42–43
   fondue, 119
   nutritional value of, 21–22
   in quiche with eggplant and red
      peppers, 132–33
   in scones with mustard and sesame,
      198–99
   Stilton, in pâté with pears, 51–52
   Stilton, in quiche with cauliflower
      and walnuts, 133–34
   straws, whole-wheat, 200
cheesecakes, 186–88
   chocolate–black-currant, 186–87
   strawberry, 187–88

chervil, in soup with apples and
  carrots, 31–32
chestnuts:
  with Brussels sprouts and wine sauce,
    84–85
  in hot sauce with brandy, 168–69
  ice cream, 167
  in nut loaf with sage and red wine,
    121
Chinese cabbage with scallions, 72, 87
chocolate:
  -almond pie, 179
  –black-currant cheesecake, 186–87
  gâteau with hazelnuts, 184–85
Christmas:
  gourmet pudding, 177–78
  vegetarian dinners for, 3–4
chunky mixed salad bowl, 74–75
cider:
  and lima bean casserole, 107–8
  in nut loaf with hazelnuts and lentils,
    122–23
  pears in, with ginger, 172
  red cabbage with apples baked in, 88
cocktail parties, 12–13
coconut and turmeric sauce, 97–98
colored pinwheels, 61–62
cookies, 189–91
  crunchy ginger, 189–90
  ginger thins, 190
  shortbread hearts, 190
  vanilla drops, 191
cottage cheese with avocados and cashew
    balls in tomato dressing, 42–43
cranberries:
  and apple sauce, 149–50
  and apples with spiced beets, 83–84
  gelatin, raspberries in, 173–74
  chilled soup with raspberries, 34–35
creamy Roquefort dressing, 157
crêpes, baked with leeks, 117–18
croquettes, potato and almond, 92–93
crudités, 50–51
crunchy ginger cookies, 189–90
cucumbers:
  braised, with walnuts, 89–90
  in salad with fennel and apples, 72–73
  and yoghurt sauce, 152
currants, black, see black currants
curried lentil balls with yoghurt and
    sour-cream sauce, miniature, 63

curried vegetable and nut pâté with
    yoghurt sauce, 54–55

desserts, 17, 159–91
  cakes, 183–85
  cheesecakes, 186–88
  cookies, 189–91
  fruit, 170–76
  ice creams, 167–69
  pies, sweet, 178–79
  puddings, 177–78
  sherbets, 163–66
  tarts, 179–82
dhal sauce, 116–17
dinner:
  Christmas, 3–4
  parties, 4–5
dips, 47–51
  Cheddar cheese and red wine, 49
  creamy lima bean, with sesame
    toast, 48–49
  sour cream and herb, with crudités,
    50–51
dressings, salad, 24, 156–59
  basil, tomatoes and lima beans in, 79
  creamy Roquefort, 157
  spicy tomato, 157
  tomato, 42–43
  vinaigrette, 156
  see also sauces

eggplant:
  fritters, with tomato sauce, 41–42
  in quiche with red pepper and
    cheese, 132–33
  ratatouille, 96–97
eggs, hard-boiled:
  bean and ripe-olive pâté with, 47–48
  and olive sandwich topping, 60–61
  sauce, 90
  vegetarian Scotch, 128–29
endive and walnut salad, 72

fats, nutritional value of, 23
fennel:
  with egg sauce, 90
  in salad with apples and cucumbers,
    72–73

festive Brussels sprouts, 85
first courses, 15–16, 40–46
flaky mushroom roll, 137–38
flour, nutritional value of, 23
fondue, cheese, 119
freezer rolls, 197–98
fruit desserts, 170–76
    apricot gelatin with fresh apricots
        and strawberries, 174
    fresh mangoes, 171
    kiwi fruit in grape gelatin, 174
    peaches in strawberry purée, 171–72
    pears in cider with ginger, 172
    raspberries in cranberry gelatin,
        173–74
    raspberry meringue gâteau, 175
    special fruit salad, 170–71
    strawberry mountain, 175–76
    stuffed pineapple halves, 172–73

garlic, 18
garlic potatoes, 95
gelatins, 25, 173–74
    apricot, fresh apricots and
        strawberries with, 174
    cranberry, raspberries in, 173–74
    grape, kiwi fruit in, 174
ginger:
    in cake with candied peel and
        almonds, 186
    crunchy cookies, 189–90
    pears in cider with, 172
    thins, 190
grapefruit rose baskets, 44–45
grape gelatin, kiwi fruit in, 174
gratin dauphinois, 91–92
green herb salad, 73–74

hazelnuts:
    chocolate gâteau with, 184–85
    in nut loaf with lentils and cider,
        122–23
herbs, 24
    bread, 195–96
    and navy bean salad, 74
    potatoes in, 93
    salad, 73–74
    and sour-cream dip, 50–51
    and sour-cream sauce, 152

stuffing, pine-nut loaf with, 123–24
    and yoghurt sauce, 152
hot avocado tarts, 56–57
hot avocado with wine stuffing, 106–7
hummus, quick, 50

ice creams, 167–69
    chestnut, 167
    raspberry, 167–68
    vanilla, with hot chestnut and
        brandy sauce, 168–69
    see also sherbets

jelling agents, 25
Jerusalem artichoke soup, 30–31
jeweled fruit tart, 181–82

kidney bean, carrot and walnut salad,
    76–77
Kir, 14–15
kiwi fruit:
    in grape gelatin, 174
    strawberry sherbet with, 166

lasagne, lentil, 143–44
leeks:
    baked crêpes with, 117–18
    in spiced vegetables with dhal
        sauce, 116–17
lemon:
    hot mayonnaise, asparagus in, 105–6
    mayonnaise sauce, 156
    pastry, black-currant lattice tart with,
        180–81
    potatoes with, 94–95
lentils:
    curried balls with yoghurt and sour-
        cream sauce, 63
    lasagne, 143–44
    and mushroom burgers, 108–9
    in nut loaf with hazelnuts and cider,
        122–23
    spaghetti with wine sauce and, 145
    spiced, 109–10
lima beans:
    and cider casserole, 107–8
    dip, with sesame toast, 48–49
    in salad with tomatoes and olives, 70

and tomatoes in basil dressing, 79
and tomato sandwich topping, 60–61
lunches, informal, 6–7

main courses, 16–17, 100–145
  baked, stuffed and en casserole,
    105–19
  nut loaves, 121–25
  pasta, 143–45
  pies, savory, 134–37
  pizzas, 141–43
  quiches, 130–34
  rissoles, 126–29
mangoes, fresh, 171
margarine, nutritional value of, 22
mayonnaise, 154–56
  blender method for, 154–55
  hot lemon, 105–6
  lemon, 156
  traditional method for, 155
melba toast, 198
melons:
  halves, with strawberries, 45–46
  sherbet with crystallized mint
    leaves, 164–65
meringue gâteau, raspberry, 175
miniature curried lentil balls with
  yoghurt and sour-cream sauce, 63
miniature open sandwiches, 60–61
molded rice and artichoke-heart salad,
  77–78
mushrooms:
  deep-dish pie, 134–36
  flaky roll, 137–38
  and lentil burgers, 108–9
  patties with yoghurt and scallion
    sauce, 58–60
  pudding, 139
  rice with almonds and red pepper,
    111–12
  in salad with tomatoes and
    avocados, 75–76
  salsify with white wine and, 114–15
  and sour-cream sauce, 151
  white nut rissoles baked with, 126

navy beans and herb salad, 74
nut loaves, 121–25

chestnut, sage and red wine, 121
lentil, hazelnut and cider, 122–23
pine-nut, with herb stuffing, 123–24
white, with capers, 124–25
nutrition, 18–24
nuts, 22–23
  cabbage salad with raisins and, 71
  nutritional value of, 22–23
  in pâté with curried vegetables and
    yoghurt sauce, 54–55
  see also specific nuts

olives:
  and bean pâté with hard-boiled eggs,
    47–48
  and egg sandwich topping, 60–61
  in salad with lima beans and tomatoes,
    70
onion rice, 99

parsnip:
  in deep-dish vegetable pie, 136–37
  root vegetables with turmeric and
    coconut sauce, 97–98
pasta, 143–45
  lentil lasagne, 143–44
  spaghetti with lentil and wine sauce,
    145
pastries, 56–60
  baby asparagus tarts, 57–58
  hot avocado tarts, 56–57
  lemon, with black-currant lattice
    tart, 180–81
  mushroom patties with yoghurt and
    scallion sauce, 58–60
pâtés, 47–55
  bean and ripe-olive, with hard-
    boiled eggs, 47–48
  curried vegetable and nut, with
    yoghurt sauce, 54–55
  Stilton, with pears, 51–53
  striped, 52–53
  walnut, en croûte, 140–41
peaches in strawberry purée, 171–72
peanuts, in salad with bananas and
  scallions, 68–69
pears:
  in cider with ginger, 172
  Stilton pâté with, 51–52

beet, apple and celery, with creamy
   topping and walnuts, 69
cabbage, with nuts and raisins, 71
carrot, apple and mint, 71–72
Chinese cabbage with scallions, 72, 87
chunky mixed, 74–75
endive and walnut, 72
fennel, apple and cucumber, 72–73
green herb, 73–74
herb and navy bean, 74
kidney bean, carrot and walnut,
   76–77
lima bean, tomato and olive, 70
molded rice and artichoke-heart,
   77–79
mushroom, tomato and avocado,
   75–76
potato, 76
special fruit (sweet), 170–71
tomatoes and lima beans in basil
   dressing, 79
salsify with white wine and
   mushrooms, 114–15
salt, 18
sandwiches, 60–62
   asparagus rolls, 62
   colored pinwheels, 61–62
   miniature open, 60–61
sauces, 24, 146–59
   apple and cranberry, 149–50
   blender Béarnaise, 153–54
   brandy butter, 158
   bread, 150
   cassis, 163–64
   coconut and turmeric, 97–98
   dhal, 116–17
   egg, 90
   hard, 158
   hot chestnut and brandy, 168–69
   hot lemon mayonnaise, 105–6
   lemon mayonnaise, 156
   mayonnaise (blender method),
      154–55
   mayonnaise (traditional method), 155
   mushroom and sour cream, 151
   sour-cream and herb, 152
   special wine, 151
   tomato, 127, 153
   wine, 84–85
   yoghurt, 54–55
   yoghurt and cucumber, 152
   yoghurt and fresh herb, 152

yoghurt and scallion, 58–60, 153
yoghurt and sour-cream, 63
see also dressings, salad
savory pies, see pies, savory
scallions:
   Chinese cabbage with, 72, 87
   in salad with bananas and peanuts,
      68–69
   and yoghurt sauce, 58–60, 153
scones, 198–99
   baby, 199
   cheese, mustard and sesame, 198–99
seasoning, 24–25
sesame in scones with cheese and
   mustard, 198–99
sesame toast, 48–49
sherbets, 163–66
   blueberry, with cassis, 163–64
   melon, with crystallized mint leaves,
      164–65
   rose, 165–66
   strawberry, with kiwi fruit, 166
   see also ice creams
shortbread hearts, 190
soft bread rolls, 196–97
soups, 27–36
   carrot, apple and chervil, 31–32
   cauliflower, with almonds, 32
   celery, 33
   chilled raspberry and cranberry,
      34–35
   green pea, with mint and cream,
      33–34
   Jerusalem artichoke, 30–31
   tomato and fresh basil, with cream,
      35–36
   vegetarian stock, 29–30
sour cream:
   baked potatoes with, 94
   filling, artichokes with, 40–41
   and herb dip with crudités, 50–51
   and herb sauce, 152
   and mushroom sauce, 151
   and yoghurt sauce, 63
spaghetti with lentil and wine sauce,
   145
special fruit salad, 170–71
special pizza, 141–42
special wine sauce, 151
spiced beets with apples and
   cranberries, 83–84
spiced lentils, 109–10

Rose Elliot, a vegetarian since the age of three, is the author of Vegetarian Dishes from Around the World. *One of England's most popular cookbook writers, she lives in Hampshire with her husband, Anthony, and her three daughters, Katy, Margaret, and Claire.*

Also by Mary B. Morrison

The Crystal Series
Baby, You're the Best
Just Can't Let Go

If I Can't Have You series
If I Can't Have You
I'd Rather Be With You
If You Don't Know Me

Soulmates Dissipate Series
Soulmates Dissipate
Never Again Once More
He's Just a Friend
Somebody's Gotta Be on Top
Nothing Has Ever Felt Like This
When Somebody Loves You Back
Darius Jones

The Honey Diaries
Sweeter Than Honey
Who's Loving You
Unconditionally Single
Darius Jones

She Ain't the One (coauthored with Carl Weber)
Maneater (anthology with Noire)
The Eternal Engagement
Justice Just Us Just Me
Who's Making Love

Mary B. Morrison, writing as HoneyB
Sexcapades
Single Husbands
Married on Mondays
The Rich Girls Club

Presented by Mary B. Morrison
Diverse Stories: From the Imaginations of Sixth Graders
(an anthology of fiction written by thirty-three 6th graders)